Mastering Gemini Prompting Artificial Intelligence for Google Workspace

Mastering Gemini Prompting Artificial Intelligence for Google Workspace

AI Prompt Guide 101
Essential Strategies for Boosting
Efficiency and Effectiveness in Business

Mindscape Artwork Publishing
Mauricio Vasquez

Toronto, Canada

Authors:
Mauricio Vasquez
Mindscape Artwork Publishing

First Printing: May 2024

ISBN-978-1-998402-34-2 (Paperback)
ISBN-978-1-998402-33-5 (Hardcover)
ISBN-978-1-998402-32-8 (E-book)

PREFACE

Welcome to a journey into the transformative world of artificial intelligence within Google Workspace. The purpose of this book, "Mastering Gemini Artificial Intelligence Prompting for Google Workspace" is to empower you, the reader, to harness AI's potent capabilities to elevate your professional activities, streamline your workflow, and achieve better outcomes in your business endeavors.

The arrival of AI technologies presents a unique opportunity for business professionals across various sectors. Whether you are a seasoned manager, a dynamic team leader, or an innovative freelancer, integrating Gemini AI into your daily processes can significantly enhance how you interact with data, manage tasks, and communicate with your team. This guide aims to provide you with the knowledge and tools to make that integration as smooth and beneficial as possible.

Artificial intelligence can seem complex and daunting. However, with the right approach, it becomes accessible and incredibly powerful. This book breaks down the barriers to understanding and utilizing AI by providing clear, concise, and practical insights into how Gemini can be leveraged within Google Workspace (Google Docs, Gmail, Google Sheets, Google Slides, Google Meet and gemini.google.com). From crafting effective prompts that drive productivity to understanding the nuanced ways AI can automate and improve tasks, this guide covers the essential skills needed to thrive in an AI-enhanced workplace.

The intent behind this book is not just to inform but to transform. By demystifying the complexities of AI, I aim to equip you with the confidence and skills to explore new possibilities and innovate within your roles. As you turn the pages, you'll discover various scenarios demonstrating Gemini's application, providing you with a practical and impactful learning experience.

Embark on this educational journey to not only enhance your technical proficiency but to become a pioneer in adopting AI within your professional landscape. Let's explore together how Gemini AI can be your partner in achieving greater efficiency and success in the digital age.

Thank you for choosing to embrace the future of productivity with this book. Your proactive step toward mastering these tools can redefine what is possible in your career and business. Let this guide be your roadmap to a more capable and efficient professional life.

Mauricio

Scan the QR code to access our book collection.

SHARE YOUR INSIGHTS

Would you spare a moment to impact someone's professional growth? Your knowledge and feedback are invaluable.

Currently, there are professionals, mentors, and leaders who are enhancing their skills and overcoming challenges. Your review could serve as a critical resource for them.

Reviews are more than just feedback; they are endorsements, shared wisdom, and a measure of trust. If you've gained actionable insights or innovative ideas from this book, please share your thoughts through a quick review. Your contribution supports:

- Guiding others to tools and strategies that enhance their leadership abilities.
- Helping individuals improve their mentoring and coaching skills.
- Broadening someone's perspective, which could be transformative.
- Inspiring changes that propel professional journeys forward.

By reviewing this book, you help expand the scope of effective leadership, mentorship, and coaching. If this book was helpful, consider recommending it to your network. The value you share can leave a lasting impression.

If you enjoyed our book, use the QR code to leave a review where you purchased it. Your feedback is crucial!

Thank you for endorsing the path to impactful leadership and personal development.

Best regards,

Mauricio

TABLE OF CONTENTS

NAVIGATING RESPONSIBILITY WITH GEMINI AI

In leveraging the capabilities of Gemini AI in Google Workspace, it's essential to recognize the dual nature of technology—it empowers and it limits. This chapter addresses your responsibility to critically assess and validate the information provided by Gemini AI and underscores the non-liability of the publisher for any consequent inaccuracies.

The Responsibility of the Reader:

Gemini AI serves as a sophisticated tool designed to enhance productivity and decision-making. However, its utility hinges on your ability to critically evaluate its output:

- Critical Evaluation: You must critically assess the relevance, accuracy, and applicability of the information provided by Gemini AI to your specific circumstances.
- Informed Decisions: While Gemini AI offers insights and suggestions, the final decisions should always rest with you, ensuring you are informed by a comprehensive understanding of the subject matter beyond the AI's contributions.

Understanding Gemini AI's Limitations:

Recognizing the limitations of Gemini AI is crucial for its effective application:

- Potential for Inaccuracy: Like any automated system, Gemini AI is susceptible to errors. These inaccuracies can stem from data misinterpretation, outdated information, or oversimplified AI models that do not capture the nuances of complex situations.
- Dynamic Information and Context: Gemini AI's knowledge is static, based on the data available up to its last training point. You should supplement AI-generated insights with the latest information and contextual understanding.

Publisher's Disclaimer:

The publisher does not guarantee the accuracy or completeness of the information generated by Gemini:

- No Liability for Inaccuracies: The publisher assumes NO responsibility for errors, inaccuracies, or omissions in the content provided by Gemini AI.
- Guidance, Not Gospel: The outputs from Gemini AI are intended as guides rather than definitive answers. You should not rely solely on this tool for critical decisions without additional verification.

Ethical Use and Accountability:

The ethical deployment of AI tools is paramount to ensure fairness, privacy, and impartiality:

- Ethical Considerations: You should consider the ethical implications of AI-generated advice, particularly in decisions that affect third parties. This involves considering data privacy, avoiding biased outputs, and promoting fairness.
- Your Accountability: Your should maintain accountability for all decisions influenced by AI insights, ensuring you can justify actions based on a balanced consideration of AI and human input.

The effective use of Gemini AI requires a symbiosis of human oversight and technological support. By understanding and embracing the responsibilities outlined in this chapter, you can enhance your engagement with Gemini AI, ensuring that you harness its capabilities responsibly and ethically to optimize your workflows within Google Workspace. The promise of Gemini AI is vast, but it is the prudent, informed, and ethical use by humans that will define its success.

WRITING EFFECTIVE PROMPTS

Since its creation, Google Workspace has enabled real-time collaboration with others. Today, this collaboration extends to artificial intelligence, integrating Gemini, designed to enhance your productivity and creativity without compromising privacy or security. Gemini's AI features enrich your experience in Gmail, Google Docs, Google Sheets, Google Meet, and Google Slides, assisting in everything from writing and organizing to streamlining workflows and enriching meetings.

This guide equips you with the core skills for crafting effective, instructional prompts using Gemini in Google Workspace. A well-crafted prompt acts as a conversation starter with your AI-powered assistant, facilitating a progressive dialogue that can continually refine outcomes. The potential applications of these prompts are extensive, yet several best practices exist to immediately enhance your productivity.

When crafting a prompt, four main components are vital. While not all need to be used simultaneously, incorporating multiple aspects often yields more precise results:

- Persona: Who is the prompt aimed at or who is acting within the prompt?
- Task: What specific task do you need help with?
- Context: What is the relevant background or situational information?
- Format: In what format should the response be presented?

Effective Prompt Crafting in Gemini for Google Workspace

Let's explore a practical example of how to construct a prompt that incorporates persona, task, context, and format effectively, particularly for use within Gmail and Google Docs:

Example Prompt for Google Workspace:

Suppose you're a Google Cloud program manager tasked with summarizing a project. You need to draft an executive summary email. Here's how you might set up your prompt:

> ✏️ You are a Google Cloud program manager. Draft an executive summary email to [project stakeholder]. Summarize key outcomes and future steps based on the attached project documents. Produce the summary in bullet points.

- Persona: You are a Google Cloud program manager.
- Task: Draft an executive summary email to [project stakeholder].
- Context: Summarize key outcomes and future steps based on the attached project documents.
- Format: Produce the summary in bullet points.

Quick Tips to Optimize Your Use of Gemini for Workspace

1. Use Natural Language: Communicate with Gemini as if you're talking to a colleague. Use full sentences and express your thoughts clearly.

2. Be Specific and Iterative: Clearly state what you need from Gemini. Whether it's summarizing information, drafting documents, or altering the tone of a communication, the more specific you are, the better the results. Don't hesitate to refine your prompts based on the responses you receive.

3. Keep It Simple: Aim for clarity and simplicity in your requests. Avoid using technical jargon unless necessary, and strive to make your prompts concise yet detailed.

4. Engage in Dialogue: Treat interactions with Gemini as a dynamic conversation. If the initial output isn't quite right, use follow-up prompts to adjust and improve the response, refining your approach based on what works and what doesn't.

By applying these principles, you can enhance your productivity and efficiency in Google Workspace, leveraging Gemini's AI capabilities to handle various tasks more effectively. This approach saves time and allows you to focus on higher-impact work that benefits from your unique expertise.

Mastering the Art of Prompting in Gemini for Google Workspace

Creating effective prompts is a nuanced skill that may require various attempts to perfect. Insights from the Google Workspace Labs program suggest that the most effective prompts are typically around 21 words long. This contrasts with the more common shorter prompts of less than nine words that many initially try.

While the potential of generative AI, like Gemini, is vast and inspiring, it's important to remember that this technology is continually evolving. As such, the responses generated can sometimes be unexpected. To ensure the best results from your prompts in Gemini for Workspace, it's crucial to review the outputs carefully for clarity, relevance, and accuracy. This step is essential because, ultimately, generative AI is designed to augment human capabilities, but the final decision and action rest with the user.

The prompts provided in this book are intended for demonstration purposes, designed to illustrate how you might structure your own prompts effectively.

Remember, the crafting of prompts is not just about achieving a single successful output but about learning through an iterative process. This approach allows you to refine and optimize prompts based on previous interactions, enhancing the AI's utility and your productivity simultaneously.

INTRODUCTION

Welcome to the world of Gemini for Google Workspace, where the fusion of generative AI with daily productivity tools transforms how you work. Integrated seamlessly with familiar applications such as Gmail, Google Docs, Google Sheets, Google Meet, and Google Slides, Gemini enhances your workplace capabilities without compromising security or privacy.

Mastering the art of prompt engineering with Gemini allows you to harness the full potential of AI to elevate your productivity and unleash your creativity. Think of Gemini as your AI-powered assistant, equipped to assist you in a variety of tasks:

- Enhancing Your Writing: Improve the clarity and impact of your text.
- Organizing Data: Streamline complex information for easy access and analysis.
- Creating Visual Content: Generate original images and graphics to complement your projects.
- Summarizing Key Information: Distill extensive data into concise, actionable insights.
- Building Connections: Foster stronger relationships with colleagues through smarter communication.
- Conducting Research: Dive into new topics quickly to gather necessary information.
- Analyzing Trends: Identify and capitalize on emerging trends and business opportunities.

This book is designed to swiftly bring you up to speed with the basic functions of Gemini, enabling you to improve day-to-day operations immediately. As you grow more accustomed to these tools, you will discover advanced prompt crafting techniques that can optimize entire workflows, positioning Gemini as a crucial partner in your professional development.

With Gemini, the possibilities to boost your effectiveness are limitless, providing you with more time to focus on strategic and impactful work. Dive into this book guide to start transforming your approach to work, leveraging Gemini to work smarter and achieve more.

How to Utilize This Prompt Guide

This is an essential handbook for mastering prompt engineering with Gemini for Google Workspace. This guide is crafted to ease you into the dynamic world of AI-powered productivity, enhancing tasks across various professional roles, including executives, founders, sales professionals, marketers, customer service representatives, project managers, and human resources specialists.

Within these pages, you'll discover a diverse array of prompt styles—some explicitly outline where to insert specific details (noted by brackets), while others provide a more general framework to show what a fully developed prompt could encompass. Every example here is designed to spark your creativity and guide your prompt crafting. However, these prompts are starting points; you'll need to adapt them to fit the precise needs of your work.

To begin, navigate to the chapter that aligns with your professional role. There, you'll find tailored prompts meant to inspire and transform your approach to daily tasks. Use these prompts to unlock new efficiencies and redefine how you engage with your work.

Exploring Gemini Features

Start exploring Gemini's capabilities by visiting the following resources. Each feature is built to integrate seamlessly with Google Workspace's robust security and privacy frameworks, ensuring that your work remains protected while you harness the full potential of AI.

- Help Me Write (available in Google Docs): Enhance your written communications with AI-powered suggestions.

- Help Me Write (available in Gmail): Enhance your emails with AI-powered improvements.

- Help Me Organize (available in Google Sheets): Streamline data management and organization tasks.

- Create Image with Gemini (available in Google Slides): Generate custom images for presentations.

- Create Background Images (available in Google Meet): Design custom backgrounds for your video calls.

- gemini.google.com Discover more about these features and begin your journey to increased productivity.

By engaging with this guide, you'll learn not just to perform tasks, but to excel in them, leveraging Gemini's advanced AI to make every workday more productive and fulfilling. As you grow more comfortable with these tools, you're encouraged to explore complex prompts that can further enhance your workflows and contribute to your professional growth.

CUSTOMER SERVICE

In the dynamic field of customer service, your goal is to offer seamless, enjoyable, and efficient support. This chapter provides practical strategies for integrating Gemini into your daily customer service operations, allowing you to standardize communication frameworks, personalize interactions, and develop new training materials—all through the power of Gemini for Google Workspace.

Getting Started

Before diving into specific prompts, revisit the general prompt-writing tips provided in the "Writing Effective Prompts" section and the foundational principles outlined in the "Introduction" of this guide. These sections equip you with the necessary tools to craft effective prompts that drive better interactions and outcomes.

Prompt Integration for Customer Service

Here, you'll find prompts paired with scenarios tailored to enhance your customer service delivery. These examples serve as a starting point for utilizing Gemini's capabilities:

1. Standardizing Communications: Learn how to create prompts that help generate standard replies for common customer inquiries, ensuring consistency across your team.

2. Personalizing Customer Interactions: Discover prompts that analyze customer data to offer personalized service recommendations or responses, enhancing customer satisfaction.

3. Creating Training Materials: Use Gemini to develop training documents tailored to new hires' needs, ensuring they receive up-to-date and relevant information.

Prompt Iteration and Refinement

Each provided prompt includes a scenario that illustrates its application, demonstrating how continuous refinement can lead to more tailored and effective communications. As you work with Gemini, you'll learn to adjust prompts better to meet the needs of your roles and tasks:

- Iterate on Feedback: Adjust your prompts based on the feedback received from both Gemini and customer interactions to refine the effectiveness of your communications.

- Expand Prompt Applications: As you become more comfortable with the basic prompts, experiment with more complex scenarios that Gemini can assist with, such as handling escalated customer issues or generating reports on customer satisfaction trends.

By integrating these AI-enhanced strategies into your customer service processes, you streamline workflows and free up valuable time to focus on more complex, high-impact tasks. This book aims to improve your efficiency and enhance the quality of your customer interactions, leveraging the advanced capabilities of Gemini for Google Workspace to transform your service delivery.

Prompt Iteration Example

Imagine you are a customer service representative dealing with a sensitive issue where a customer has received damaged goods. To address this, you decide to use Gemini within Google Docs to draft an empathetic and constructive response. Here's how you could structure your prompt:

1. Open Google Docs: Start a new document and click on the "Help me write" feature.

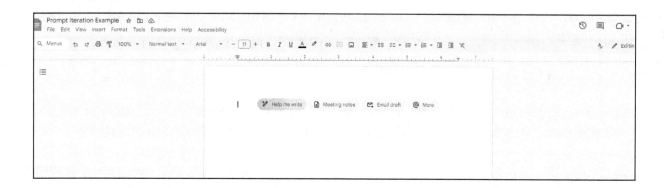

2. Craft Your Prompt: Enter the following prompt to Gemini:

> "Help me craft an empathetic email response. I am a customer service representative, and I need to create a response to a customer complaint. The customer ordered a pair of speakers that arrived damaged. They've already contacted us via email and provided pictures of the damage. I've offered a replacement, but they're requesting an expedited shipping option that isn't typically included with their order. Include a paragraph that acknowledges their frustration and three bullet points with potential resolutions."

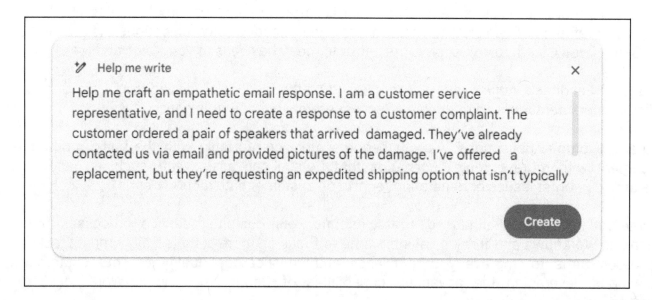

After clicking "Create" you will get the following in Google Docs:

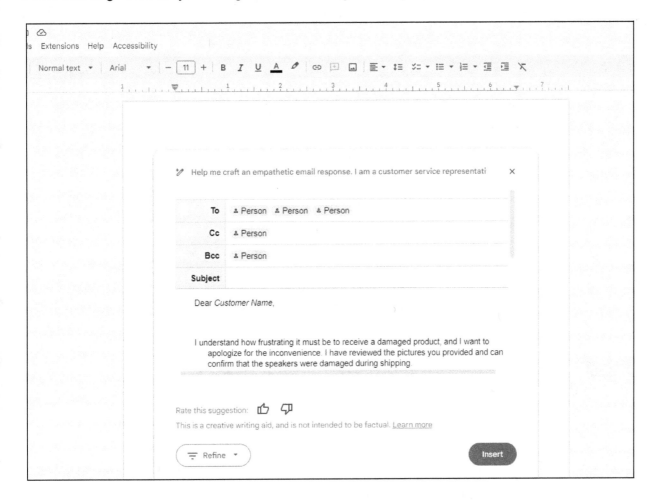

You like the email that Gemini in Docs created so you select "Insert". But you want to brainstorm ways to resolve the issue without offering expedited shipping. You prompt by selecting "Help me write" and you type:

"Suggest 10 alternative options in place of expedited shipping to resolve the customer's frustration about receiving the damaged package."

Here is this process step by step:

Step 1:

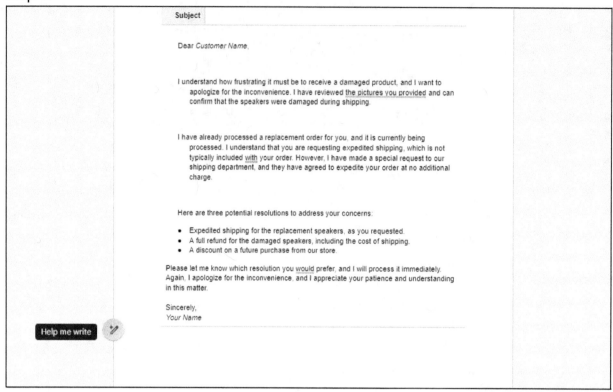

Step 2:

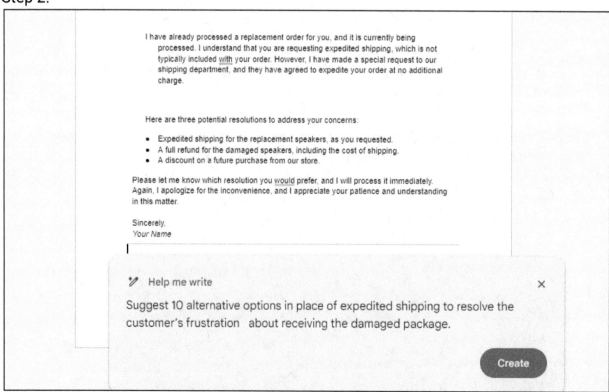

Step 3:

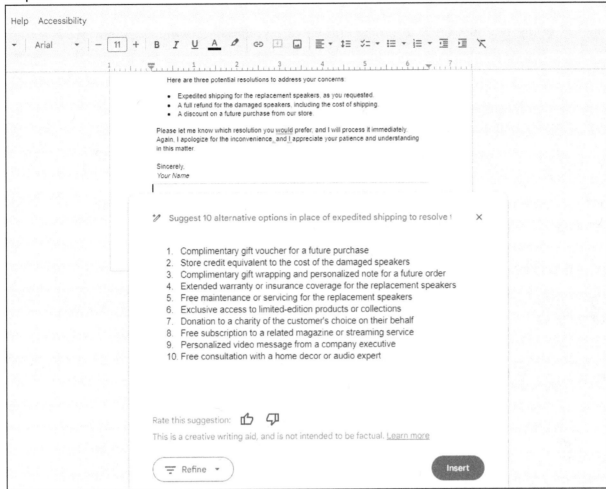

These 10 suggestions are helpful, so you click "Insert" to add the text to your draft.

This example showcases how to use Gemini to transform a standard customer interaction into an opportunity to enhance customer satisfaction. By structuring your prompt to include specific details about the situation, you ensure that the generated response is both relevant and considerate. This method not only streamlines the response process but also helps maintain a high standard of customer service by effectively and empathetically addressing the customer's concerns.

Tips for Effective Prompt Engineering in Customer Service:

- Be Specific: Clearly outline the context of the customer's issue to generate a response that is directly applicable and highly relevant.
- Show Empathy: Ensure that the prompt's tone directs Gemini to produce content that reflects understanding and care for the customer's situation.
- Offer Solutions: Structure the prompt to not only acknowledge the issue but also to explore feasible solutions, demonstrating proactive customer service.

By following these guidelines, you empower yourself to create responses that address the immediate concerns and enhance the overall customer experience, leveraging the capabilities of Gemini in Google Workspace to optimize and elevate your service interactions.

Prompt Guide

Customer Service Manager or Representative
Use Case: Standardizing Communication Frameworks

As a customer service manager overseeing a growing team, your challenge lies in standardizing communication to maintain a consistent and professional tone across all customer interactions. To address this, you can harness the capabilities of Gemini in Google Workspace, specifically using Google Docs for prompt crafting.

Step-by-Step Prompt Crafting Guide:

1. Open Google Docs: Initiate a new document where you will create your communication templates.

2. Use Gemini's "Help me write" Feature: Click on "Help me write" and input your specific requirements for communication templates:

    "Compose templates for three types of customer communications: apology emails, order confirmation messages, and thank-you notes for loyal customers. Each template should be concise, limited to one paragraph, and maintain a friendly and accommodating tone."

3. Refine and Customize: Once Gemini generates the initial templates, review them to ensure they align with your company's branding and tone. Make necessary adjustments to better suit your specific context and requirements.

4. Develop Communication Best Practices: To enhance your team's efficiency and consistency further, draft a document outlining best practices for customer interactions. Again, use Gemini to assist. You open a new Google Doc and prompt Gemini in Docs with the following:

    "Develop a comprehensive list of communication best practices that we can use to train new team members. Outline three sections including how to handle happy customer inquiries, neutral customer inquiries, and dissatisfied customer inquiries."

5. Develop Standardized Language for Communication: You also want to help your team with standardized language that they can use when interacting with customers on phone calls. You want to brainstorm, so you open gemini.google.com and type:

✦ *"I am a [customer service manager]. I am creating a standardized language that my team can use when interacting with customers during phone calls. Produce templates for common call openings, greetings, and closures for a customer service representative at a retail store. These templates should allow for the personalization of customer details. The goal is to ensure consistency and professionalism while allowing for differentiation with specific customer information."*

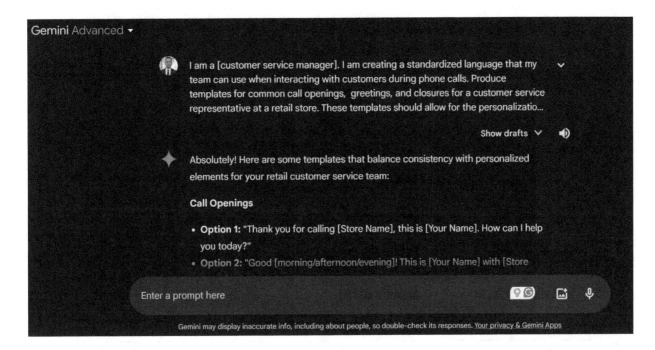

6. Implement and Train: With these templates and best practices in place, integrate them into your team's onboarding and training programs to ensure all members can effectively apply these standards in their daily interactions.

This method not only simplifies creating and standardizing communication across your team but also ensures that all customer service representatives are equipped with tools to handle various customer sentiments efficiently. By leveraging Gemini's AI capabilities, you can ensure that your team responds to customer needs and enhances satisfaction and loyalty through consistent and empathetic communication.

Use Case: Improve customer service

With a rise in customer complaints, engaging various departments to enhance the customer experience effectively becomes essential. Starting with the key stakeholders, you decide to use Gemini in Gmail to facilitate the initial communication.

Step-by-Step Process to Draft an Email Using Gemini:

1. Open Gmail: Navigate to your Gmail account and compose a new email.

2. Activate Gemini: Select the "Help me write" option within Gmail.

3. Enter Your Prompt: Type the following request to Gemini:

✏️ *"Compose an email inviting marketing, sales, and product team leaders to a meeting next week. The purpose is to discuss and improve our customer experience strategies. Please outline the importance of defining clear roles and responsibilities."*

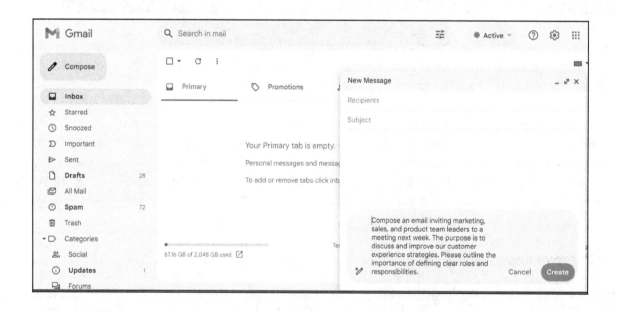

4. Review and Customize: After Gemini drafts the email, review it to ensure it aligns with your tone and company's communication standards. Make necessary adjustments to personalize the message further and click "Insert".

5. Send the Email: Once finalized, send the email to the respective department leads, initiating the collaborative process.

Creating a Tracking Spreadsheet

Next, to keep track of the initiatives and their outcomes, you decide to create a structured spreadsheet.

Steps to Create a Spreadsheet Using Gemini in Google Sheets:

1. Open Google Sheets: Start a new spreadsheet for tracking the initiatives.
2. Activate Gemini: Use the 'Help me organize' feature in Sheets.

3. **Enter Your Prompt:** Provide Gemini with the specifications for your tracking tool and click "Create"

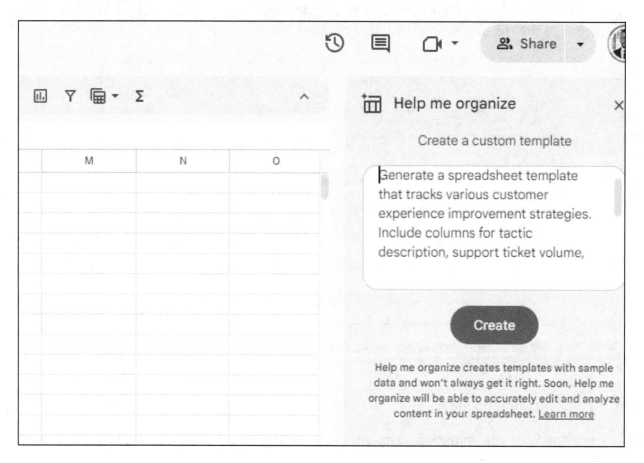

4. **Review and Adjust:** Review the generated spreadsheet to ensure it meets your requirements. Customize the format or add additional metrics as necessary.

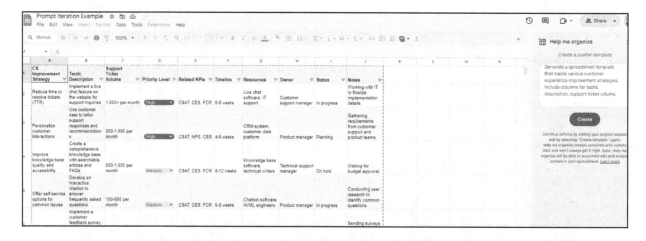

5. **Implement the Template:** Use this template to document ongoing efforts and outcomes from the cross-departmental strategies. This tool will be instrumental in visualizing progress and making data-driven decisions.

By leveraging Gemini in Google Workspace, you streamline the process of initiating and managing cross-departmental collaboration aimed at improving customer satisfaction. These steps not only facilitate effective communication but also ensure ongoing tracking and management of improvement initiatives, making your approach to customer experience both strategic and systematic.

Customer Support Specialist

Use case: Enable customer self-service

As a customer support specialist, addressing common queries effectively is crucial. Given that your team frequently receives questions regarding return policies, and customer feedback indicates confusion, it's essential to clarify these guidelines.

Creating Clear Policy Documents Using Gemini

1. Start with the Existing Documents: Open your current document that includes detailed information about return, refund, and store credit policies in Google Docs.

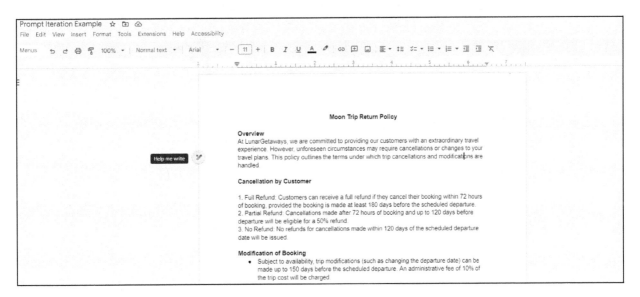

2. Use Gemini to Simplify Information: Activate the "Help me write" feature in Google Docs, input the following prompt and click "Create":

"Simplify this document to outline our product return policy clearly. Please provide a concise summary and list 5 actionable steps for customers to follow sequentially."

Moon Trip Return Policy

Overview

At LunarGetaways, we are committed to providing our customers with an extraordinary travel experience. However, unforeseen circumstances may require cancellations or changes to your travel plans. This policy outlines the terms under which trip cancellations and modifications are

---

✐ Help me write   ✕

Simplify this document to outline our product return policy clearly. Please provide a concise summary and list 5 actionable steps for customers to follow sequentially.|

Create

Modification of Booking

- Subject to availability, trip modifications (such as changing the departure date) can be made up to 150 days before the scheduled departure. An administrative fee of 10% of the trip cost will be charged.

3. Refine and Repeat: Review the simplified steps provided by Gemini, ensuring they are clear and easy to follow. Apply the same process to summarize your refund and store credit policies.

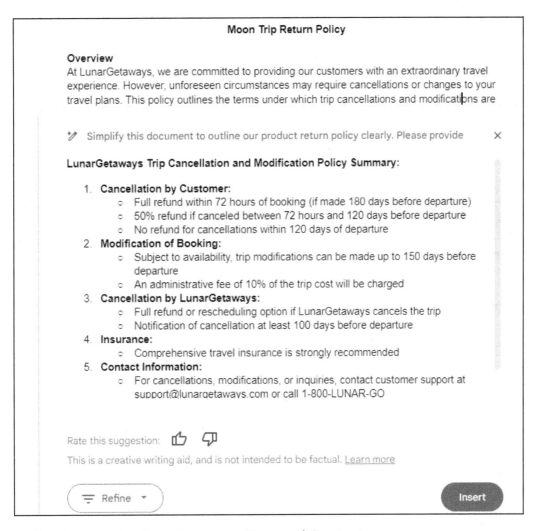

Transforming Policy Summaries into Customer-Focused Content

With the simplified content, the next step is to communicate these policies effectively to your customers through a blog post:

1. Draft a Blog Post: Using the refined policy documents, prompt Gemini again to help transform this information into an engaging blog post. The prompt might look like this:

"Convert the summarized return, refund, and store credit policies into a blog post titled 'Resolve Common Issues Without Agent Assistance'. Organize the content into separate sections for each policy."

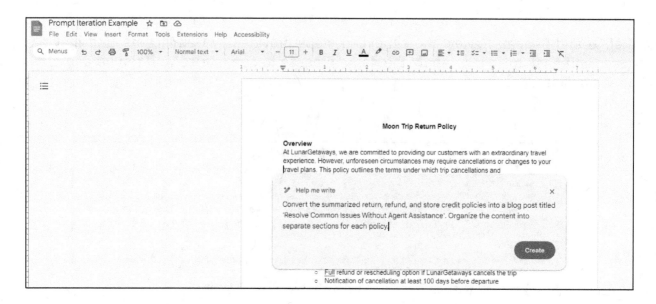

2. **Ensure Accessibility and Engagement:** Make sure the blog is not only informative but also engaging, helping customers understand how they can address issues independently, which enhances their experience and reduces dependency on direct support.

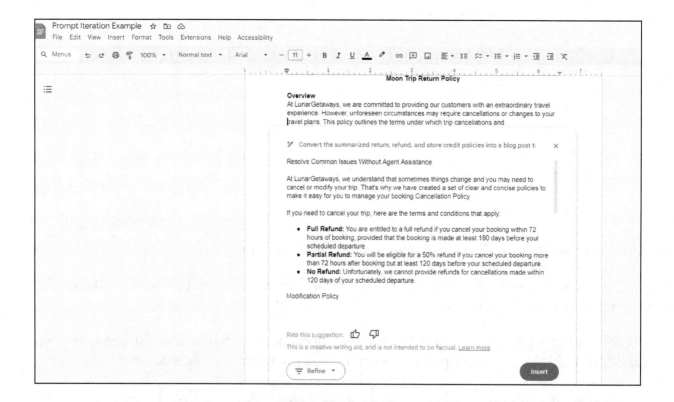

Creating an Email Template for Direct Communication

Finally, to assist customers who reach out directly, create an email template that guides them toward self-service resources:

1. Draft an Email Template: Use Gemini to draft a template that can be used when responding to inquiries related to these policies. The prompt could be:

✏️ *"Create an email template that directs customers to our new blog post on self-service options for returns, refunds, and store credits. Include a link to the blog, thank the customer for their business, and emphasize our commitment to their satisfaction."*

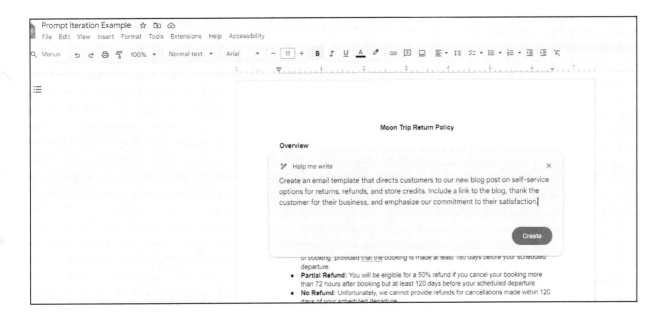

2. Customize and Personalize: Review the template to ensure it reflects the brand's voice and commitment to customer service, making necessary adjustments to personalize the communication further.

Use Case: Voice of the customer research

In response to the new company policy of directly engaging dissatisfied customers, you employ Gemini in Gmail to handle customer complaints more effectively. Here's how to optimize your communication to ensure it's constructive and responsive.

1. Open the Customer's Email: Start by reviewing the complaint to understand the specifics of the customer's dissatisfaction.
2. Activate Gemini's "Help me write" Feature: In Gmail, use the prompt feature to draft an initial response. Input the following prompt:

✏️ *"Compose an email requesting a follow-up conversation with the customer who provided negative feedback about [reason for the complaint]. Propose date and time for the discussion, and suggest potential solutions to their issue."*

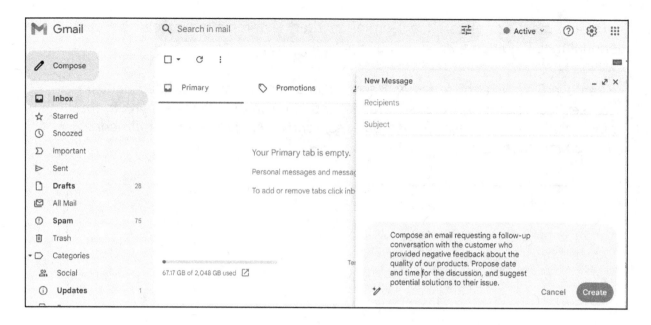

3. Refine the Language: Given the sensitivity of addressing complaints, if the initial draft is too direct, use the 'Refine > Elaborate' option in Gemini to soften the tone, making it more empathetic and understanding.

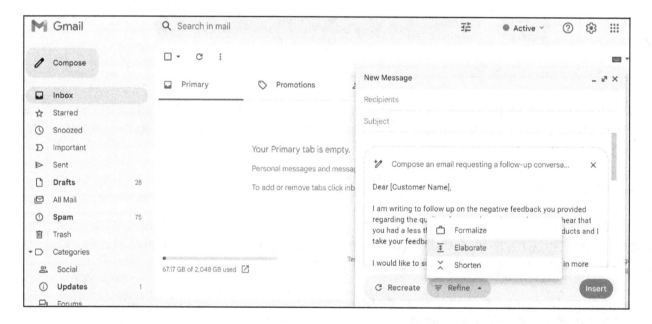

Developing a Post-Call Survey to Measure Effectiveness:

To further enhance customer service, creating a feedback mechanism is essential. Here's how you can use Gemini in Google Docs to develop a survey that measures the effectiveness of your follow-up calls:

1. Create a New Document: Open Google Docs to start a new document for your survey.
2. Prompt Gemini for Survey Questions: Use the following prompt to generate relevant survey questions:

"Generate a survey with five questions aimed at customers who have recently interacted with our support team over the phone. These questions should assess the effectiveness of the conversation, inquire whether their concerns were addressed, and determine their likelihood of recommending our services."

3. Review and Customize the Survey: Once Gemini provides a draft, review the questions to ensure they are clear, unbiased, and effectively measure customer satisfaction. Adjust as needed to align with your company's feedback goals.

Once your survey is finalized, incorporate it into the standard follow-up routine. Send this survey to customers after each support call to gather valuable insights that can inform and improve your customer service strategies.

Client Services Coordinator
Use case: Engage with customers

As you refine your company's policies and align them with your customer's needs, engaging directly with your most loyal customers through a listening tour is a strategic move. Here's how you can use Gemini in Google Workspace to facilitate this process, ensuring clarity and professionalism throughout your communications.

1. Compose the Invitation Email: Open Gmail and initiate a new email. Use the "Help me write" feature by selecting it in the options.
2. Draft the Invitation: Enter a prompt into Gemini to help draft an inviting and informative email:

"Compose an email to invite our most loyal customers to a feedback session. Include details about the location, date, and time, emphasizing the focus on discussing updates to our [policies]."

3. Personalize and Send: Review the draft to ensure it conveys warmth and appreciation for the customers' continued support. Personalize the message further if necessary, then send it to your selected customer base.

Responding to Feedback After the Listening Tour

After hosting the session and gathering valuable insights, it's crucial to follow up with attendees to show appreciation and outline next steps.

1. Follow-up with Thank You Notes: Open Gmail again and prompt Gemini for assistance in crafting personalized thank you emails.
2. Craft the Thank You Note: Use this prompt to generate tailored messages:

"Write a personalized thank you note for [customer name], appreciating their valuable input during our feedback session. Mention how their suggestions will contribute to refining our policies and the expected improvements."

3. Personalize Each Response: Insert the specific names and any particular feedback from each attendee to personalize the messages. This shows genuine appreciation and reinforces the value of their input.

Benefits of Using Gemini for Customer Engagement

- Efficiency: Quickly generates drafts for communications, saving time and allowing you to focus on personalizing interactions.
- Consistency: Maintains a professional and uniform tone across all communications, which is crucial for building trust and credibility with your customer base.
- Engagement: Enables personalized follow-ups, enhancing customer relations and demonstrating your commitment to incorporating their feedback.

Use case: Prepare for client meetings

As you take on a new client in an unfamiliar industry, it's crucial to approach your initial meetings with a well-prepared and informed perspective. Here's how to use Gemini in Google Workspace to effectively prepare and engage with your new customers.

Researching the Industry with Gemini

1. Initiate Research: Open gemini.google.com to gather detailed information about the customer's industry. Use Gemini's advanced AI capabilities to help draft your research questions:

"Generate five insightful questions to deeply understand the challenges and dynamics within the [industry] industry. These questions should help me grasp the main issues this industry faces."

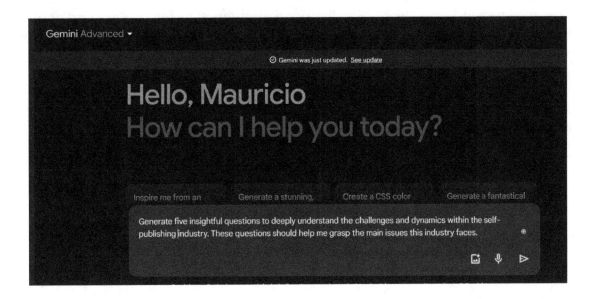

2. Deepen Your Understanding: Use the questions provided by Gemini as a foundation for further discussions with the tool. As you explore these questions, note down key insights and additional queries that arise.
3. Compile Research Notes: Gather all your findings and discussions into a Google Doc for easy reference and organization.

Summarizing Key Points for Discussion

Once you have compiled comprehensive notes, it's time to distill them into clear, actionable talking points:

1. Summarize Findings: With the detailed notes in your Google Doc, use Gemini to help condense this information into a digestible format:

"Summarize the key findings from these notes about the [industry] and generate concise talking points that I can discuss during my meeting with the client."

2. Review and Refine: Ensure that the summary captures all critical aspects and effectively highlights the main points of interest that are relevant to your customer.

Crafting Your Introduction Email

With your preparation complete, you are ready to formally introduce yourself to the client and set up your first meeting:

1. Compose an Introduction Email: Open Gmail and use the "Help me write" feature to draft an introductory email. The prompt should be carefully tailored to establish a connection:

"Draft an introductory email where I present myself as the new client services coordinator for [account]. Propose a meeting to discuss [specific topic], and request their availability within the next two weeks."

2. Personalize and Send: Customize the generated email to reflect your personal style and the formal tone suitable for professional interactions. Make sure it invites dialogue and expresses eagerness to understand and meet the client's needs.

By leveraging Gemini in Google Workspace, you streamline your preparation process for important meetings, ensuring you are well informed and ready to make a great impression. This approach enhances your efficiency and boosts your confidence by having a solid foundation of knowledge and prepared points to discuss.

EXECUTIVES AND ENTREPRENEURS

As an executive or entrepreneur, your role demands not only strategic vision but also the ability to execute at a rapid pace. Each decision you make influences your organization's growth, innovation, and direction. Staying informed about market trends and making well-informed strategic decisions are crucial.

Equally important is managing your tasks efficiently, especially when you are away from your desk. This guide section explores how Gemini for Google Workspace can empower you with AI-generated prompts that enhance decision-making, improve business outcomes, and streamline your tasks.

Getting Started

1. Introduction to AI-Powered Efficiency: Before diving into specific prompts, familiarize yourself with general prompt-writing techniques. Understanding these basics will help you effectively communicate with Gemini to maximize the AI's capabilities.
2. Customizable Prompts for Diverse Executive Needs: Each example prompt below is accompanied by a scenario illustrating how you might use Gemini in your executive workflow. These prompts are designed to be adjusted according to your specific needs to help manage tasks, gain insights, and facilitate collaboration.

Prompt Iteration Example

As an executive, managing communication effectively, especially regarding board meetings, is crucial. Here's how you can use Gemini in Google Workspace to streamline your communication while preparing for an upcoming board meeting during a tight schedule.

Drafting a Strategic Email Using Gemini in Gmail

1. Open Gmail: As you prepare to board your flight, open Gmail on your device to address the upcoming board meeting.
2. Activate Gemini's "Help me write" Feature: Select this feature to assist in composing your email efficiently.
3. Compose Your Email: Input the following instructions into Gemini to create a concise yet comprehensive email:

> ✏️ *"Draft an email to confirm my attendance at the next board meeting. Propose an addition to the agenda to discuss [urgent topics] for 15 minutes, highlighting their importance to our strategic goals. Provide the email in short paragraphs."*

- Task: *Draft an email*
- Context: *to confirm my attendance at the next board meeting. Propose an addition to the agenda to discuss [urgent topics] for 15 minutes, highlighting their importance to our strategic goals.*
- Format: *Provide the email in short paragraphs.*

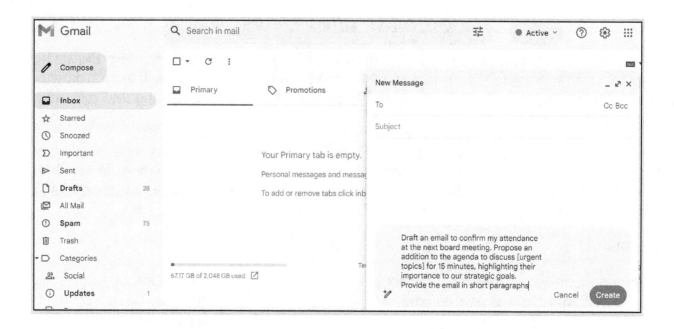

4. Personalize and Finalize: Review the draft provided by Gemini, making any necessary adjustments to personalize the message or add specific details about the urgent topics. Ensure the tone remains professional and that the email effectively conveys the significance of the added agenda items.

The email looks good, but you want to ensure the tone is as formal as possible. To do this, select "Refine" > "Formalize." You read the revised email and select Insert. Before sending it, you make a light edit to thank the team for keeping you on track.

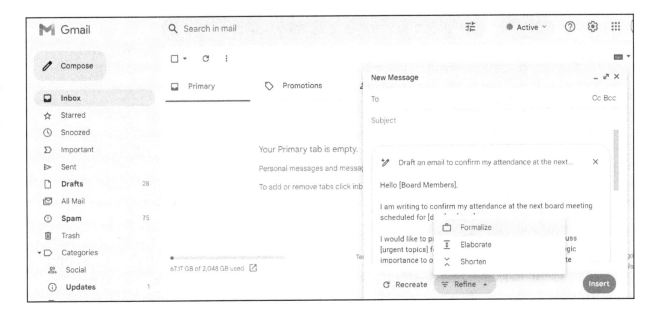

Ensuring Effective Communication

This approach not only saves you time but also ensures that your communication is clear, direct, and aligned with your executive role's demands. By leveraging Gemini to handle routine but important tasks, you can focus on strategic thinking and decision-making, even while in transit.

Benefits of Using Gemini for Executive Tasks

- **Efficiency:** Quickly generates well-structured emails, allowing you to communicate effectively with limited time.
- **Clarity:** Ensures all communication is clear and aligned with your organizational objectives, enhancing decision-making processes.
- **Strategic Alignment:** Helps maintain focus on critical issues by incorporating them into meeting agendas, ensuring they receive the necessary attention.

Prompt guide

Chief Operating Officer
Use case: Preparing for the town hall meeting

As an executive offer preparing for a crucial quarterly town hall, it's essential for you to communicate effectively and sensitively to address both achievements and setbacks. Here's how Gemini can facilitate crafting impactful, empathetic communications and streamline responses during busy schedules.

1. Brainstorming Tough Questions and Responses:

Navigate to gemini.google.com and type the following prompt:

◆ *"I'm the COO and am preparing for a quarterly town hall. Despite positive progress, some teams are disheartened due to unforeseen setbacks. Help me craft challenging questions that employees might ask about our earnings, leadership changes, and future vision. Also, suggest responses that convey confidence yet firmness."*

Review and adapt the generated questions and responses to prepare thoroughly for potential inquiries during the town hall.

2. Developing Empathetic Responses:

The questions and suggested answers have effectively laid the groundwork for your preparation. Now, you aim to refine how you can respond with empathy, particularly during uncertain times. To explore this further, you engage Gemini once more. You enter the following prompt:

◆ *"These questions and responses are a good start. Now, help me refine responses to emphasize empathy and reassurance, letting employees know we are committed to improvement and collective success."*

3. Crafting Uplifting Opening Remarks:

You want to work backwards from these questions to come up with uplifting remarks you can share at the open the town hall. You decide to brainstorm with Gemini in Docs. Create a new document, select "Help me write", and write the following prompt:

✏️ *"Craft two uplifting opening paragraphs for the town hall, recognizing the past quarter's challenges while highlighting the positives that lie ahead. The tone should be motivating, optimistic, and promote unity."*

Streamlining Responses on the Go

Your schedule has unexpectedly shifted due to an urgent task, preventing you from attending the upcoming meeting. To make sure the team is still well-informed on critical points, you open Gmail and utilize a voice command to activate Gemini. You say:

1. Managing Sudden Schedule Changes:

Open the Gmail app in your mobile and active the voice command:

Use the voice command to say:

✐ *"Draft an email to [project lead] explaining my absence from today's meeting due to an urgent matter. Request detailed notes be taken and decisions on [key topic] be made, assigning the postmortem report to [colleague]."*

How Gemini Enhances Executive Functioning

- Efficiency: Quickly drafts emails and documents, saving time and allowing for focus on strategic decision-making.
- Precision: Tailors communications that resonate with both company culture and the specific nuances of employee sentiments.
- Adaptability: Offers the ability to promptly adjust to changing schedules and communicate changes effectively.

Chief Marketing Officer
Use case: Brainstorm content and thought leadership

As a Chief Marketing Officer, harnessing the power of Gemini for Google Workspace can transform your approach to content creation, brand campaigning, and competitive analysis. Here's how you can effectively leverage Gemini's capabilities to enhance your marketing strategies and communications.

1. Generating Blog Post Ideas:

After a productive discussion with your social media team, you've compiled extensive notes on what resonates with your audience, including trending topics and effective keywords.

In your existing Google Doc, activate Gemini by selecting "Help me write" and input the prompt:

> ✏️ *"Generate a list of four compelling thought leadership blog post ideas for [company] based on current trending topics, our target audience analysis, and key brand keywords."*

2. Developing a New Brand Campaign:

Recognizing the need for a fresh brand campaign that highlights your company's reliability and innovation,you open a new Google Doc, select "Help me write" and type:

> ✏️ *"Generate three slogan options that emphasize reliability, innovation, and our long-standing popularity, suitable for [company]."*

3. Designing Trade Show Booth Graphics:

With upcoming events, creating a visually appealing booth is crucial. In Google Slides, select "Create image with Gemini" and provide the following details:

> 🖼️ *"Design a modern trade show booth in orange and blue, incorporating interactive computer stations that reflect our brand's innovative spirit."*

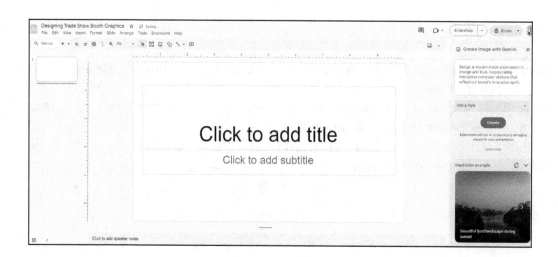

Conducting Competitive Analysis

1. Analyzing Competitors for Business Expansion:

Considering expanding into a new line of business and needing a quick, insightful competitive analysis, visit gemini.google.com and input:

- *"I am a CMO conducting competitive analysis as we consider entering [new line of business]. List the top five competitors in the [industry], detailing their pricing, strengths, weaknesses, and target demographics."*

2.

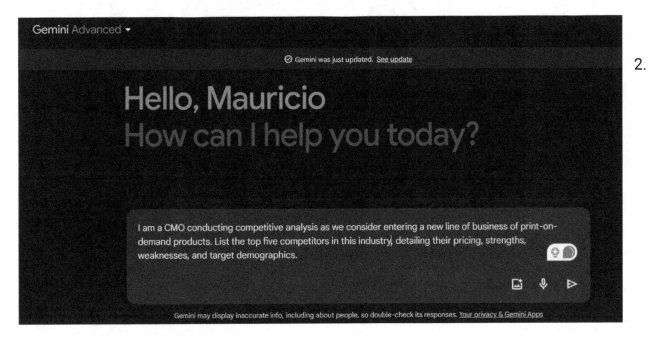

Crafting a Competitive Strategy:

Following deeper research, you aim to draft a strategic plan to persuade your CEO about the new business venture. Continue on gemini.google.com with the prompt:

- *"Draft a concise five-year competitive strategy for entering [line of business] in North America, outlining key goals, strategies, and tactics."*

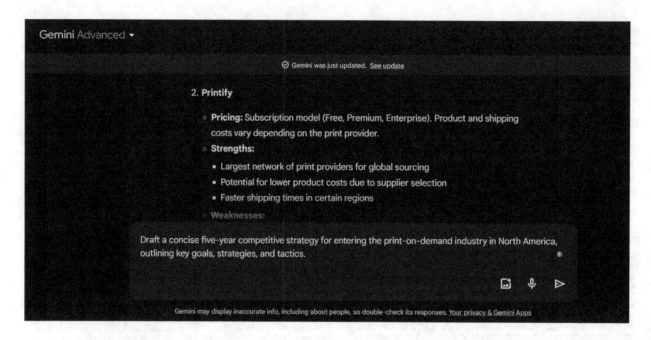

2. **Printify**

○ **Pricing:** Subscription model (Free, Premium, Enterprise). Product and shipping costs vary depending on the print provider.

○ **Strengths:**

- Largest network of print providers for global sourcing
- Potential for lower product costs due to supplier selection
- Faster shipping times in certain regions

○ Weaknesses:

Draft a concise five-year competitive strategy for entering the print-on-demand industry in North America, outlining key goals, strategies, and tactics.

By integrating Gemini into your workflow, you can efficiently generate innovative ideas, strategically analyze competitive landscapes, and produce engaging marketing materials. This not only saves time but also ensures that your strategies are grounded in data-driven insights, enhancing your ability to lead and innovate within the marketing domain.

Chief Technology Officer
Use case: Summarize emerging technology trends

As a Chief Technology Officer, staying updated with the rapidly evolving technology landscape is crucial. To efficiently capture the most relevant emerging trends, you utilize Gemini in Google Workspace. Here's how you can effectively gather and apply this vital information:

1. Initiating Research:

Open gemini.google.com and type in the following prompt:

✦ *"As the CTO of [company] within the [industry], I need a concise summary of the top five emerging technologies that could significantly impact our sector. Please provide the potential benefits and challenges of each technology, along with insights on how they might influence our company in the next two to three years."*

2. Analyzing the Summary:

The initial summary Gemini provides will serve as a foundational overview, helping you identify key areas for deeper investigation.

3. Deepening the Research:

To expand on specific points of interest, continue the dialogue with Gemini:By leveraging

Gemini for Google Workspace, you can efficiently synthesize vast

✦ *"Based on the initial summary, recommend three strategic areas where [my organization] should focus to stay ahead in [specific technologies or trends]."*

amounts of information into actionable insights, enabling you to lead your organization effectively through technological changes. This tool allows you to focus on strategic implementation rather than getting bogged down by the vast data, ensuring your actions are informed and impactful.

Chief Information Officer
Use case: Develop technical communications

As a Chief Information Officer, you often face the challenge of conveying complex technical information succinctly, especially to busy executives like the CEO. Here's how you can utilize Gemini within Google Workspace to streamline these communications effectively.

1. Summarizing Key Technical Findings:

After receiving a detailed report on the company's security posture, you need to present the core information in a digestible format. Open the Google Doc containing the report and select "Help me write." Then, input the following:

✐ *"Summarize the key findings and implications of this report for [audience]. Highlight the main vulnerabilities identified and the recommended actions to address them, ensuring the summary maintains a formal tone."*

Use the concise summary as an executive summary to top the detailed report, making it accessible for quick understanding by the CEO.

2. Scheduling a Strategic Discussion:

With the summary ready, the next step is to discuss these findings in detail. Open Gmail, select "Help me write" and type:

✐ *"Draft an email to the CEO requesting a 30-minute meeting next week to discuss strategic IT changes, emphasizing the importance of scalability, security, and data management in our upcoming initiatives."*

Tracking IT Assets

1. Creating a Software License Tracker:

There is an immediate requirement to monitor software access for new hires effectively. Open

Google Sheets, select "Help me organize," and enter:

> ▦ *"Create a spreadsheet to track software licenses for employees. Include columns for license types, usage rights, and renewal dates to ensure comprehensive management of IT assets."*

By leveraging Gemini, you can enhance both the efficiency of internal processes and the effectiveness of your communications. This tool allows you to:

- Simplify complex information: Quickly condense detailed reports into executive summaries that capture essential information.
- Facilitate strategic discussions: Efficiently arrange meetings with top executives to discuss critical IT developments.
- Optimize asset management: Streamline the tracking of IT assets, ensuring all information is up-to-date and easily accessible.

Chief Human Resources Officer
Use case: Demonstrate employee appreciation

As a Chief Human Resources Officer, you're dedicated to fostering a culture of appreciation and understanding within a large organization. Here's how you can effectively use Gemini in Google Workspace to develop programs that make every employee feel valued and heard.

Developing Employee Appreciation Programs

1. Brainstorming Appreciation Ideas:

To create a comprehensive appreciation program that caters to diverse interests, you open a new Google Doc, select "Help me write" and type:

> ✐ *"Generate 10 creative employee appreciation ideas that align with our company culture of [type] and cater to varied interests like cooking, gardening, sports, reading, and traveling."*

Use Gemini's ideas to initiate interest clubs and events that promote engagement and a sense of community within the company.

2. Creating Inspirational Email Templates for Leadership:

Gemini in Docs has sparked your creativity, and you now have some ideas for employee interest clubs and events. To promote consistent recognition of team talent by your leadership, you decide to create inspirational email templates. You activate Gemini in Docs by selecting "Help me write" and you enter:

"Compose an email template that managers can use to thank employees for their exceptional efforts and [recent accomplishments]. Include a gesture of appreciation such as a coffee gift card, maintaining an upbeat and professional tone."

Use case: Assess employee satisfaction

1. Drafting an Employee Satisfaction Survey:

You've noticed that your team seems overwhelmed recently. Before meeting with your direct reports, you plan to create an anonymous survey to gauge their honest feelings. To formulate the questions, you open a new Google Doc, select "Help me write" in Gemini in Docs, and type:

"Create an anonymous employee satisfaction survey focusing on workload, work-life balance, compensation, and career growth. Ensure the questions are clear, unbiased, and comprehensive."

2. Summarizing Survey Results:

You have received feedback from 15 senior leaders and compiled all the anonymous responses in a Google Doc. To prepare for your next call, you need a concise summary. You open Gemini in Docs, select "Help me write" and type:

"Summarize the key themes from the employee feedback to highlight major insights that will inform our discussion on enhancing workplace satisfaction."

Leveraging Gemini in these applications allows you to:

- Enhance Employee Engagement: By recognizing diverse interests and achievements, you strengthen workplace morale and commitment.
- Streamline Communication: Email templates facilitate consistent and heartfelt recognition from leadership, reinforcing a culture of appreciation.
- Improve Workplace Satisfaction: Detailed analysis of survey results helps address concerns effectively, fostering a supportive and understanding work environment.

Founder or Entrepreneur
Use case: Develop a competitive analysis

As a startup founder, your business is gaining momentum online, and you're now contemplating the leap into a brick-and-mortar store. To make an informed decision, you decide to use Gemini to analyze the competitive landscape thoroughly.

Conducting a Detailed Competitive Analysis

1. Understanding the Current Market:

To get a clear view of the competitive dynamics before opening a physical store, you navigate to gemini.google.com and input the following prompt:

✦ *"I am the founder of a startup considering a transition to a brick-and-mortar store. Conduct a detailed analysis of the competitive landscape focusing on [specific focus area]. Outline the strengths and weaknesses of [key competitors], their strategies, tactics, and outcomes. Provide actionable insights and recommendations for how [my company] can refine its strategy and secure a competitive edge."*

2. Deepening Competitive Insights:

You've collected valuable insights from your session with Gemini at gemini.google.com. To delve deeper into your analysis of two specific competitors, you type:

✦ *"Generate a detailed competitive analysis comparing [my company] with [competitor] within the current market. Highlight key differentiators and potential strategic advantages."*

3. Organizing Findings for Strategic Planning:

To compile and review the data for strategic discussions and planning, transfer the insights gathered from your discussions with Gemini into a new Google Doc for easy reference and further analysis.

Using Gemini, you can:

- Identify Market Opportunities: Understand the broader market dynamics and how your business can uniquely position itself in a competitive retail environment.
- Refine Business Strategies: Use detailed competitor analyses to refine your approach, ensuring your entry into the brick-and-mortar space is well-planned and capitalized on existing strengths.
- Streamline Decision-Making: Quickly gather and organize critical data to support fast and informed decision-making as your business grows.

Use case: Conduct fundraising and investor relations

As you prepare to transition your business to a brick-and-mortar store, securing investor support is crucial. Here's how you can use Gemini in Google Docs to effectively communicate with potential investors, from the initial outreach to follow-up communications.

1. Drafting an Initial Email to Investors:

You're prepared to contact potential investors to launch your brick-and-mortar store. To craft an introductory email, you open the Google Doc containing your notes and research. Using Gemini in Docs, you select "Help me write" and enter:

- *"Create a personalized email template for potential investors that showcases [company's] unique value proposition and recent advancements in [initiatives]. Include a request for a meeting within the next month to explore potential collaborations."*

The generated template serves as a foundational draft. Customize it with specific details and a personal touch to resonate more effectively with each potential investor.

2. Thanking Investors Post-Meeting:

After a promising discussion with potential investors, it's important to maintain momentum and address any outstanding questions or concerns. Open the Google Doc containing notes from your meeting. Use Gemini to draft a follow-up by selecting "Help me write" and entering:

- *"Compose a thank you email to the investor who participated in our recent discussion. Express appreciation for their time and interest. Propose scheduling a follow-up meeting to delve deeper into [specific questions and concerns] they raised."*

Leveraging Gemini for Effective Communication

By integrating Gemini in your fundraising and investor relations efforts, you benefit from:
- Efficiency in Communication: Quickly generate well-structured initial and follow-up emails that are tailored to the context of each investor interaction.
- Enhanced Personalization: Easily adjust the drafts to include specific details that make your communications feel personal and thoughtful.
- Strategic Follow-Up: Ensure continuity in engagement by promptly addressing investor feedback and advancing the conversation towards securing investment.

Use case: Manage time off policies and tracking

As part of enhancing workplace productivity and clarity for new hires, simplifying the presentation of your company's time-off request policy is essential. Additionally, efficiently tracking weekly staffing for shift-based employees is crucial. Here's how you can utilize Gemini in Google Workspace to manage these tasks effectively.

Simplifying Time Off Request Policies

1. Creating a User-Friendly Policy Guide:

To make the time-off request policy accessible and understandable for new hires, open the Google Doc containing your company's handbook. Select "Help me write" in Gemini in Docs and type:

"Create a straightforward, step-by-step checklist that outlines the company's time-off request policy, ensuring it is written in plain language to be easily understood by all employees."

This action transforms complex policy language into a clear, concise checklist that new hires can easily follow, facilitating a smoother onboarding process.

2. Implementing a Staffing Management System:

To maintain an organized overview of weekly staffing, crucial for managing shift-based employees effectively. Open Google Sheets, click on "Help me organize," and input:

"Generate a table to monitor weekly staffing levels. Include columns for date, name, shift (AM or PM), and notes to ensure all relevant details are captured."

This spreadsheet becomes a vital tool for overseeing staffing arrangements, allowing for real-time adjustments and ensuring operational efficiency.

By employing Gemini to refine internal processes such as policy dissemination and staffing management, you can:

- Enhance Clarity and Accessibility: Convert detailed policy documents into easy-to-digest formats that enhance comprehension and compliance.
- Streamline Operations: Quickly create practical tools for managing essential HR tasks, reducing administrative burdens and allowing more focus on strategic activities.

HUMAN RESOURCES

As a Human Resources professional, you play a crucial role in shaping the culture and operations of your organization. Managing confidential information, recruiting talent, and ensuring a positive employee experience are key responsibilities that require efficient handling. This section guides you on using Gemini in Google Workspace to streamline your HR tasks effectively.

Integrating Effective Prompts in HR Operations

To enhance productivity and optimize time management in HR-related activities, start by familiarizing yourself with the basic prompt-writing techniques outlined at the beginning of this guide. Learning to craft effective prompts can significantly speed up your daily tasks, from recruiting to onboarding.

Use Gemini to automate and improve various HR processes:

- Recruiting: Kick-start your recruiting process by generating job descriptions or screening questions tailored to specific roles.
- Onboarding: Simplify the onboarding process with customized welcome emails and essential document checklists.
- Culture Building: Foster a culture of belonging through regular engagement prompts and feedback surveys.

Each prompt in this section is accompanied by a scenario illustrating how HR professionals can use Gemini for different tasks. These examples serve as a blueprint for adapting Gemini to meet your needs. The guide also demonstrates how to iterate on prompts based on initial results, ensuring that each subsequent output better meets your requirements.

Getting Started

Review general prompt-writing tips provided early in this guide to understand the fundamentals of effective communication with Gemini. Explore the scenarios provided to gain insights into how tailored prompts can be employed in practical HR situations, enhancing your efficiency and effectiveness.

Prompt Iteration Example

As an HR manager tasked with creating a welcoming onboarding experience, you need to prepare an engaging presentation script for new hires that highlights your company's dedication to employee development and well-being. Here's how you can utilize Gemini in Google Docs to streamline this process:

Crafting a Presentation Script Using Gemini in Google Docs:

1. Opening Your Working Document: Start by opening the Google Doc that contains your accumulated notes, bullet points, and topics intended for the new hire orientation.

2. Initial Prompt to Gemini: Activate Gemini in Docs by selecting "Help me write" and input the following prompt:

"I'm an HR manager developing a script for a new hire presentation. I need to emphasize our company's commitment to employee development and well-being. Please help me create talking points that highlight why mentorship and development are fundamental to our company values."

- Persona: *I'm an HR manager*
- Task: *I need to emphasize our company's commitment to employee development and well-being.*
- Context: *developing a script for a new hire presentation*
- Format: *Please help me create talking points that highlight why mentorship and development are fundamental to our company values.*

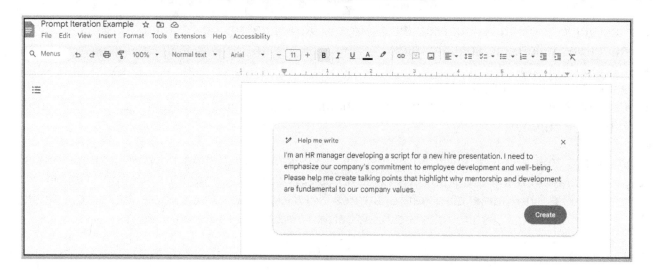

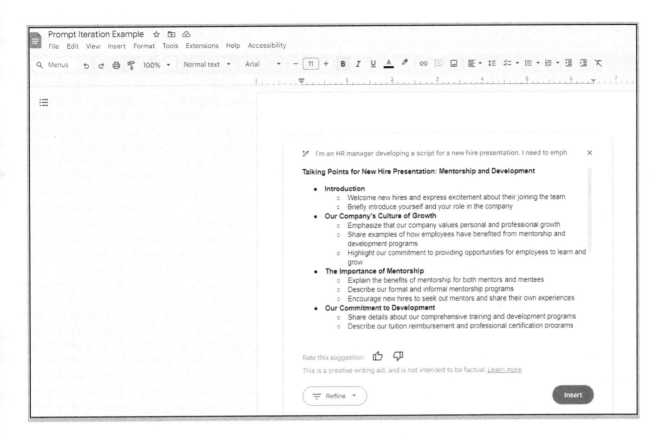

You're pleased with what Gemini in Docs produced, so you choose "Insert" to add it to your document. Next, you want to refine your talking points. You highlight sections of your Google Doc that discuss training and certification programs and mentorship opportunities, and then you type:

"Create four talking points for a new section of the presentation script that outline how we support employee development. Include details about our training and certification programs and mentorship opportunities."

Company Commitment to Employee Development and Well-being

- Our company is committed to the personal and professional growth of our employees.
- We believe that mentorship and development are essential to our success.
- We offer a variety of programs and resources to support employee development, including:
  - Formal mentorship program
  - Tuition reimbursement
  - Professional development stipends
  - Access to online learning resources
  - Opportunities for on-the-job training
- We encourage our employees to take advantage of these opportunities and to actively seek out ways to grow and develop their skills.
- We believe that by investing in our employees, we are investing in the future of our company.

Benefits of Mentorship and Development

- Mentorship and development can help employees:
  - Improve their job performance
  - Advance their careers
  - Develop new skills and knowledge
  - Increase their job satisfaction
  - Build stronger relationships with their colleagues
- Mentorship and development can also help the company by:
  - Increasing employee retention
  - Boosting employee morale
  - Improving productivity
  - Fostering innovation

  - Professional development stipends
  - Access to online learning resources
  - Opportunities for on-the-job training
- We encourage our employees to take advantage of these opportunities and to actively
  ...v and develop their skills.
  ...vesting in our employees, we are investing in the future of our

| Development

...opment can help employees:
...job performance
...careers
...skills and knowledge
...job satisfaction
...relationships with their colleagues
...opment can also help the company by:
...ployee retention
...loyee morale
...ductivity
...vation

Tone

Summarize

Bulletize

Elaborate

Shorten

Rephrase

Create four talking points for a new section of the presentation script that outline how we support employee development. Include details about our training and certification programs and mentorship opportunities. →

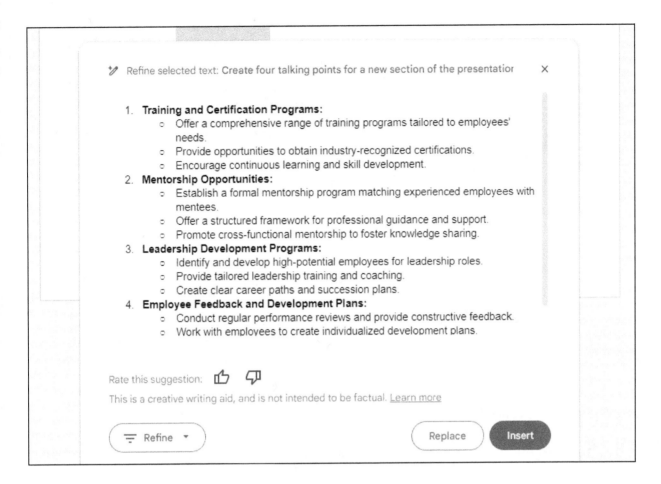

You click "Insert" to add the content. Next, you're looking to craft a compelling conclusion for your script. You highlight notes on expected team behaviors in the Google Doc and prompt Gemini in Docs by typing:

"Compose a strong closing statement that emphasizes our expectation for everyone to contribute to a respectful and welcoming workplace, maintaining a professional tone."

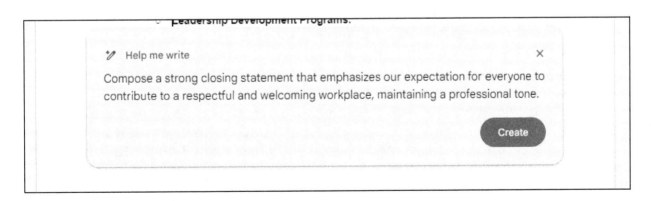

In closing, I want to emphasize the importance of creating a respectful and welcoming workplace for everyone. Our company values diversity and inclusion, and we expect all employees to contribute to a positive and professional atmosphere. By treating each other with respect, we can create a workplace where everyone feels safe, valued, and supported. Thank you for your commitment to our company and our shared values.

Rate this suggestion: 👍 👎

This is a creative writing aid, and is not intended to be factual. Learn more

Prompt guide

Recruiter
Use case: Manage the recruiting process

As your business expands and your hiring needs increase, you decide to optimize the recruiting process. You open the team's "Recruiting Strategies" Google Doc, which contains notes on strategies, channels, and templates for candidate outreach. Using Gemini in Docs, you select "Help me write" to begin brainstorming improvements and type the following prompt:

1. Initial Brainstorming Session:

Open the "Recruiting Strategies" Google Doc, and use Gemini in Docs by selecting "Help me write" and input:

> ✏️ *"Develop a list of enhanced strategies for our recruiters to better manage the recruitment process and identify potential candidates."*

2. Creating Role Descriptions:

After drafting recommendations for recruitment improvements, your team needs to urgently hire a Social Media Marketing Manager skilled in B2B and B2C content, with at least ten years of experience and a portfolio of social media posts. You open a new Google Doc and initiate Gemini in Docs to craft the job description.

> ✏️ *"Draft a detailed job description for a Social Media Marketing Manager focusing on key responsibilities and requirements such as B2B and B2C content creation, at least ten years of experience, and a portfolio of work."*

3. Refining the Job Description:

After Gemini generates a draft, review and tweak the content for clarity and appeal. To further refine the description you use the following prompt:

"Enhance this job description to make it more attractive to prospective candidates, focusing on our company's unique opportunities and the specific attributes of the target audience.

Use case: Manage the interview process

1. Preparing Interview Questions:

Before conducting phone screen interviews, you decide to draft some questions. You visit gemini.google.com and write:

"I am a recruiter preparing for candidate interviews. Write a list of 20 open-ended questions for [open role URL] that can be used to screen candidates effectively."

2. Summarizing Interview Notes:

Post-interview, you have a Google Doc filled with detailed notes from each discussion. To condense this information, you prompt Gemini in Docs:

"Summarize the interview notes and generate a shortlist of top candidates for the [position]."

3. Communicating with the Hiring Manager:

With the interviews summarized, you aim to inform the hiring manager about the candidates. In the same Google Doc, you prompt Gemini by selecting "Help me write", and you type:

"Generate an email to the hiring manager summarizing the profiles of [candidates]."

Use case: Candidate communication

1. Communicating Offers to Selected Candidates:

After finalizing the hiring decisions, you access the candidate notes in a Google Doc and activate Gemini in Docs by selecting "Help me write" to assist with drafting communications. To create an offer letter template, you type:

> *"I am preparing an offer letter for a candidate who recently completed the interview process. Using Gemini in Docs, create a template for the [selected candidate] for the [position], which includes a request to schedule a call to discuss benefits, compensation, and the potential start date."*

2. Handling Rejections with Empathy:

Next, you focus on crafting considerate rejection letters for those not selected. To create a personalized and empathetic rejection email, you prompt Gemini in Docs by selecting "Help me write" and typing:

> *"Compose a rejection letter for [candidate] who were not selected for the [position]. Ensure the tone is empathetic and supportive."*

HR Manager
Use case: Onboard employees

1. Onboarding New Employees:

As an HR manager overseeing the onboarding of new hires, it's crucial to organize their first week to ensure a smooth transition. Utilizing Gemini in Google Sheets, you set up a detailed schedule. In Google Sheets, activate Gemini by selecting "Help me organize" and prompt:

> *"Create a table that details a new employee's first-week schedule, highlighting key meetings, training sessions, introductions, and includes a column for key contacts and priority levels (low, medium, high)."*

This results in a formatted spreadsheet ready to be customized with specific details, utilizing conditional formatting to categorize tasks by priority through color coding.

2. Fostering Team Integration:

Next, to promote team bonding for the new hires, you brainstorm activities that encourage collaboration. Open a new Google Doc and engage Gemini by selecting "Help me write" and submitting the following prompt:

> *"Design a team-bonding activity, like an office scavenger hunt, for team members to collaborate during their meeting."*

Gemini provides creative suggestions which you then fine-tune and validate with the team lead.

3. Welcoming New Team Members:

To effectively communicate with new hires about their initial meeting, you use Gemini in Gmail. Simply open Gmail, activate Gemini by selecting "Help me write," and enter your message:

✐ *"Draft an email to the new employees on the [team] to introduce them to the rest of the team and outline the objectives of the upcoming team-building session."*

Use case: Communicate key findings and draft follow-up surveys

1. Streamlining Executive Communications:

Post-onboarding, your focus shifts to ensuring company research is comprehensible for leadership and supportive of a welcoming environment for skill development. You prompt Gemini in Docs by selecting "Help me write". You type:

✐ *"Draft an email to senior leadership summarizing key findings from our [report], starting with an introductory paragraph and followed by bullet points highlighting the crucial insights."*

Gemini in Docs provides a bullet-pointed summary which you refine before emailing it to the leadership team.

2. Evaluating Policy Impact

For your next step, to gauge how recent policy changes have affected the employee experience, you open Gemini in Docs, select "Help me write," and start drafting a survey with the following prompt:

✐ *"Create an anonymous employee survey with questions about workload, work-life balance, and career growth to assess the impact of recent company policy changes."*

MARKETING

As a marketing professional, your role is central to driving compelling campaigns, enhancing brand experiences, and generating leads. You excel in harnessing data-driven insights, crafting engaging messages, and deeply connecting with audiences. This section equips you with streamlined methods to integrate prompts into your daily activities. Mastering prompt writing boosts your productivity, allowing you to reclaim time to dedicate to strategic initiatives. Explore how to effectively utilize prompts to unleash creativity, automate insights, and develop impactful campaigns through Gemini for Google Workspace. For Chief Marketing Officer-specific scenarios, refer to the Executives and Entrepreneurs section of this guide.

Getting Started

Begin by reviewing general prompt-writing tips at the start of this guide. Each prompt is paired with a scenario, providing context for effectively engaging with Gemini for Workspace. These examples show how to progressively build on your initial prompts to refine and tailor outputs to suit various marketing functions. Adjust these prompts to streamline your daily tasks and enhance your campaign results.

Prompt iteration example

As a brand manager and owner of a consulting firm, you're tasked with establishing a visual identity for a client's new venture—a fusion restaurant that blends Asian and Latin cuisines. To begin conceptualizing the brand's logo, you turn to Gemini for assistance. Accessing gemini.google.com, you type:

✦ *"Generate creative logo ideas for a new business that combines Asian and Latin cuisines. Consider the following in the design:*

1. *Dual Concept: The logo should seamlessly integrate elements from both Asian and Latin culinary traditions without appearing too cluttered.*
2. *Target Audience: Design with a diverse audience in mind, catering to food enthusiasts who appreciate innovative and fusion dishes.*
3. *Style Options: Explore three different design approaches for comparison:*
   - *Modern and Playful: Utilize vibrant colors and engaging graphics, possibly incorporating cultural symbols in a stylized form.*
   - *Retro-Cool: Channel a vintage diner vibe with bold, chunky typography and warm, inviting colors.*
   - *Sleek and Minimalist: Focus on clean lines and geometric shapes for a subtle nod to both culinary traditions."*

This structured approach will help you generate distinct, appealing logo options that effectively represent the fusion of Asian and Latin cuisines while appealing to your client's broad target audience.

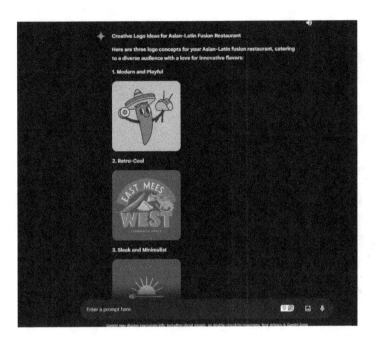

You like the retro-cool option. You continue your conversation by typing:

✦ *" I like the retro-cool option. Provide three more in that same style."*

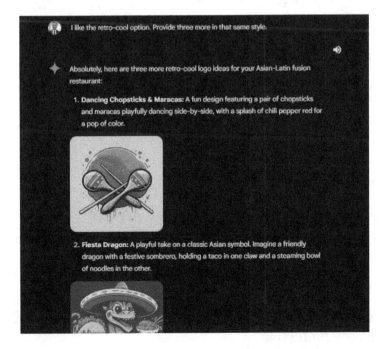

Now that you have some logo ideas, you're ready to brainstorm business names and a tagline. You type:

> ✦ *"Generate a tagline and 10 potential business names for the logo 'Fiesta Dragon'"*

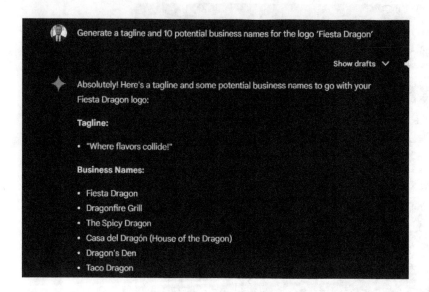

Prompt guide

Brand Manager
Use case: Conduct market research and identify trends

In a rapidly evolving industry, staying ahead of market trends is crucial. To facilitate timely and efficient market research, you turn to Gemini at gemini.google.com and enter the following prompt:

> ✦ *"I am conducting market research on the [industry] to identify new trends. Use [URLs] to extract information on emerging trends and shifting consumer preferences."*

Ad Copy Variation for A/B Testing

Once you've synthesized the research findings, your team decides to refresh your brand's campaign messaging. To determine the most effective approach, you plan to A/B test various ad copy versions. At gemini.google.com, you specify your need:

> ✦ *"We are updating our campaign messaging and want to A/B test its effectiveness. Here's our current message: [messaging]. Please generate three diverse ad copy variations for testing."*

Use Case: Content creation and distribution management

As your customer navigates exciting leadership transitions, you're tasked with crafting a compelling narrative to highlight these changes. Starting with a blog draft, you leverage Gemini in Google Docs to streamline your content creation:

> *"Generate a blog draft announcing that [name] has joined [company] as [position]. Include details such as their previous roles at [former company], notable achievements, and active contributions to professional organizations."*

Streamlining Content Distribution Tracking

To effectively manage where and how this new content is shared, you need a robust tracking system. You open Google Sheets and use Gemini to create a structured tracker:

> *"Create a project tracker for monitoring content distribution. Include columns for distribution channel, responsible party, URL, and priority level (low, medium, high)."*

Digital Marketing Manager

Use Case: Customer acquisition communications

Email remains a crucial channel for engaging directly with your prospects and customers. To jumpstart your new email campaign, open a new Google Doc and utilize Gemini in Docs by selecting "Help me write":

> *"Generate three distinctive email subject lines targeting [audience segments] that highlight our [product]. Ensure the lines are engaging yet maintain a professional tone."*

Collaborating with the Copywriting Team

Once you've crafted your subject lines, it's essential to get feedback from your team to refine them further. To facilitate this, you switch to Gmail, and using Gemini, you draft a concise communication by selecting "Help me write" and writing:

> *"Compose a brief email to the copywriting team presenting the [suggested email subject lines]. Ask for their input by week's end and express appreciation for their contributions."*

Use Case: Developing inbound marketing campaigns

Your team has just completed a new ebook tailored for executives, exploring best practices with your latest solution. Now, you're tasked with creating a landing page to promote this gated content effectively. Open a new Google Doc and engage Gemini by selecting "Help me write" Input your request:

> ✦ *"Compose engaging copy for a landing page that promotes our new [ebook/webinar/free trial], specifically designed for an executive audience. Emphasize the key benefits and drive conversions with compelling calls to action."*

Nurturing Leads Through Email Campaigns

With the landing page up and the campaign live, your next step is to nurture the leads who downloaded the ebook. Again, use Google Docs integrated with Gemini by selecting "Help me write":

> ✦ *"Create content for a series of five automated emails intended to nurture leads who have engaged with our [ebook topic]. Personalize the emails by including [recipient's name] and promote further interaction with additional resources or exclusive offers."*

Content Marketing Manager
Use case: Generate inspiration for your blog

As the content marketing manager for a travel company's blog, you aim to differentiate your content in a crowded market. Start by engaging with Gemini at gemini.google.com for brainstorming. Select "Help me write" and input the following:

> ✦ *"I need blog post topics that stand out in the travel and tourism industry. Focus on unique angles and current trends or recent innovations within the sector. Include:*
>
> - *Target Audience: Define the specific demographic each topic will appeal to.*
> - *Content Outline: Provide bullet points detailing the main ideas for each blog post.*
> - *Call to Action: Suggest an engaging way to involve the reader at the end of the post."*

Creating Compelling Visual Content

Following the brainstorming success, your next step involves visual content creation to complement your blog posts. Open a new Google Slide and engage Gemini by selecting "Create image with Gemini" with the prompt:

"Generate an image of a plane soaring above clouds, mountains, and rivers at sunrise for our travel company's marketing campaign."

Use case: Create social media posts

As someone responsible for social media content, your goal is to create engaging posts tailored to specific audiences. You open a new Google Doc and prompt Gemini in Docs by selecting "Help me write" and typing:

"Compose three concise social media posts about [product/service/topic] for [target audience]. Limit each post to two sentences and include a call to action directing readers to [our website]."

Promoting Events on Social Media

Next, to generate buzz for an upcoming event aimed at recent graduates, open a new Google Doc and prompt Gemini in Docs by selecting "Help me write" and writing:

"Generate a social media post to promote our upcoming [event name]. Use compelling language and incorporate relevant hashtags to capture the attention of [audience]."

Use case: Create a strategic marketing plan

Your company is launching an innovative app, and you need to craft a detailed marketing strategy. To initiate this process, interact with Gemini via gemini.google.com. Input your prompt:

"I'm crafting a marketing strategy for a new app focused on [functionality] targeting [audience]. I need a comprehensive plan emphasizing [marketing channels]. Please include a competitor analysis, optimal marketing channel mix with justifications, budget suggestions, key messaging strategies, and a proposed campaign timeline with KPIs."

Communicating Strategic Insights to Leadership

With the insights gathered, you're now ready to compile these into a high-level document for your CMO. Open Gmail and utilize Gemini's assistance by selecting 'Help me write' and entering:

"Prepare an email draft for the CMO outlining that I will submit a concise strategic marketing plan for the upcoming app launch by [date]. This document will feature an executive summary, analysis of the competitive environment, primary marketing channels, and the targeted demographics for South American markets."

PROJECT MANAGEMENT

As a project manager, you orchestrate complex, dynamic projects, ensuring they meet their objectives efficiently. Gemini for Google Workspace offers tools to streamline your project management activities, enhancing your ability to plan, execute, and deliver projects with precision. This section will guide you on harnessing Gemini's capabilities to optimize your workflows, boost efficiency, and improve project outcomes.

Getting Started

Begin by exploring the prompt-writing tips. These foundational skills will help you effectively interact with Gemini.

Each prompt included below is paired with a practical scenario, illustrating how Gemini can be integrated into your project management processes. These examples will help you understand the potential applications of Gemini in real-world settings.

Learn to build on initial responses from Gemini. This iterative approach allows you to refine outputs and tailor them to meet the specific needs of your projects. Adjust prompts as needed to ensure they align with your project goals and deliver actionable insights.

Prompt iteration example

After successfully completing the registration form for a new website, the next crucial step involves creating User Acceptance Tests (UATs) to ensure the form functions correctly across different scenarios. This process is essential for validating that the form meets all user requirements and technical specifications before it goes live. Visit gemini.google.com and type:

> ✦ *"Generate a table outlining 10 User Acceptance Tests for our latest website registration form, ensuring each test addresses a different aspect of the form's functionality."*

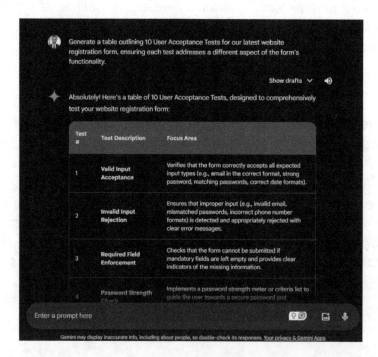

You find the results to be a useful beginning, so you export them to a Google Sheet. Next, you need to communicate the next steps to your colleague who is managing the User Acceptance Tests (UATs). You open gemini.google.com and type:

✦ *"Draft an email to [my colleague], who is responsible for the UATs, explaining the next steps they need to take for the UAT process."*

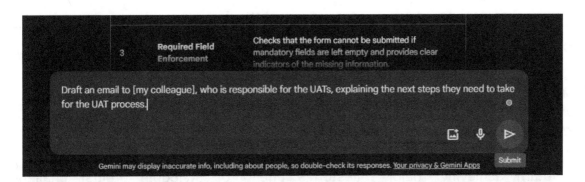

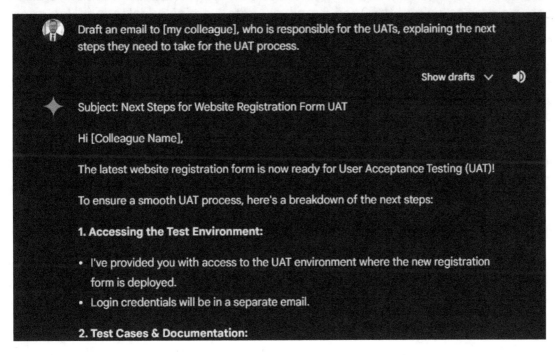

The drafted email serves as a good starting point, so you export the results to Gmail and make direct edits before sending it to your colleague.

Prompt guide

Project Manager
Use case: Report on project status

After a detailed discussion with your project stakeholders, you need to consolidate and communicate the key points and action items. Open your Google Docs, where the meeting transcript is saved, and use Gemini by selecting "Help me write". Enter:

> *"Provide a concise summary of this call in one paragraph. List the action items, decisions made, and assignees for each task based on [call transcript]."*

Next, to keep your manager informed about recent developments, you decide to standardize your project update communications. In a new Google Doc, activate Gemini and input:

> *"Create a template for project status updates to my manager, including sections for this week's key achievements, any obstacles encountered, and the top three priorities for the following week."*

With your team achieving major milestones ahead of schedule amidst challenging circumstances, it's time to celebrate. Open Gmail, activate Gemini by selecting "Help me write" and type:

> *"Compose an invitation for a team lunch to acknowledge our project's progress, specifying [date, time, and location]. Express gratitude for the team's dedication and recognize the challenges overcome."*

This method ensures your communications are not only timely but effectively maintain the momentum of your project and team morale.

Use case: Create a project retrospective

You've successfully concluded a major project and it's time for a thorough review. Your task is to provide the senior leadership team with a comprehensive project retrospective. Begin this process by opening a Google Doc and activating Gemini by selecting "Help me write." Input the following:

> *"I need to compile a detailed retrospective report on [project]. Please create a list of 20 questions that will guide a thorough review across all teams involved. The questions should aim to identify what aspects were successful, pinpoint areas of failure, and explore any issues related to processes, technical elements, communication gaps, or other factors that influenced the project's outcome."*

After Gemini in Docs generates a foundational set of questions, review and refine them to ensure they meet your specific needs. Share the document with your team to collect their insights. Once you have gathered sufficient feedback, it's time to draft the retrospective report. Again, use Gemini in Docs and type:

> *"Condense the feedback from this document into two comprehensive paragraphs. Summarize the project's objectives, key players, outcomes, notable achievements, and any significant challenges encountered."*

This approach helps you efficiently collate and present the retrospective analysis, ensuring that all critical information is communicated clearly and effectively to your leadership, thereby facilitating better planning and execution for future projects.

Use case: Develop an issue tracker and related communications

As you prepare to manage projects effectively, creating a robust issue tracker is crucial for monitoring project risks and resolving them promptly. To start, open a new Google Sheet and engage Gemini by selecting "Help me organize." Input your request:

> *"Generate a spreadsheet to monitor project issues, which should include columns for the issue description, current status, the responsible party, and detailed action steps for resolution."*

With the project's preliminary phase approaching, it's essential to have standardized communication templates ready. For addressing arising issues, open a new Google Doc and prompt Gemini by selecting "Help me write." Type in your request:

> *"Create an email template that can be used to report issues. The template should detail the issue's causes, potential solutions, and expected resolution timelines."*

After reviewing the initial template and finding it satisfactory, you decide to prepare for more critical situations. Still in the same Google Doc, prompt Gemini again:

> *"Compose a second email template, this time for escalating serious project issues to stakeholders. The email should clearly outline the issue's impact and suggest immediate solutions."*

This structured approach not only streamlines creating necessary project management tools but also ensures that all communication remains clear, professional, and actionable, enabling you to maintain control over the project lifecycle and enhance overall responsiveness.

In the fast-paced world of sales, understanding your customers thoroughly is the key to success. You handle critical relationship management, interpret buying signals, design customized solutions, and make strategic, data-informed decisions.

Gemini for Google Workspace is here to transform your productivity and strengthen your client relationships. This section is dedicated to offering you practical prompts and scenarios tailored for sales professionals, enhancing your daily operations and allowing you more time to focus on what truly matters—your customers.

Getting Started

Before you dive in, familiarize yourself with the foundational prompt-writing techniques found at the beginning of this guide.

Each prompt included below comes with a scenario to inspire effective collaboration with Gemini in Workspace. These examples show how you can continually refine prompts to improve their effectiveness and customize them to meet specific sales tasks:

1. Prompt Iteration Example: Learn to iteratively refine your prompts to enhance their precision and relevance, ensuring that every interaction with Gemini leads to more accurate and useful outputs.
2. Role-Specific Examples: Discover how different roles within the sales team can utilize Gemini to streamline workflow, from generating leads to closing deals.

By mastering these prompt-engineering skills with Gemini, you'll unlock new levels of efficiency and insight, enabling you to dedicate more time to cultivating valuable client relationships.

Prompt iteration example

You're an account executive who has just been assigned to a new client and you're looking to make a strong first impression. You need to introduce yourself and start building a relationship with the key contacts at the client's company. To do this, you decide to send an introductory email. You open Gmail and use Gemini to assist you by selecting "Help me write." You enter the following prompt

"Draft an email to [name], the new [title] at [company]. In the email, congratulate them on their new position, introduce yourself as their main contact at [your company name], and invite them to lunch next week to discuss synergies. Ask if they would prefer to meet on Monday or Tuesday."

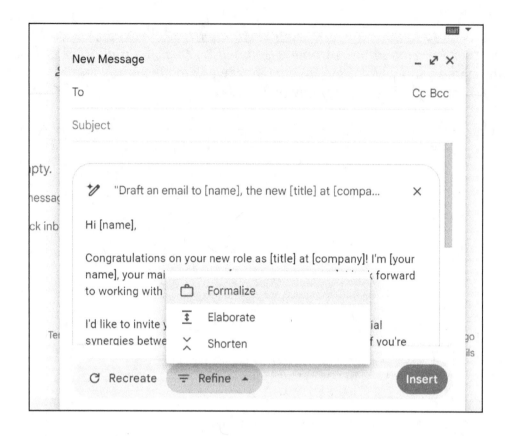

This gives you a solid foundation, but you're aiming for an even more polished response. You click on "Refine > Formalize" to enhance the quality.

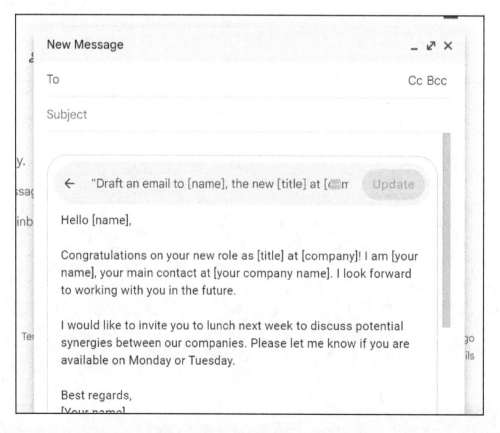

You're satisfied with the email, so you click "Insert." After reviewing the message one final time and making some minor edits, you send it off.

Next, you want to delve deeper into understanding the customer and their marketing strategies. To start your research, you visit gemini.google.com and type:

✦ *"I am an account executive responsible for [customer name]. I need to conduct initial research on [customer]'s market strategy."*

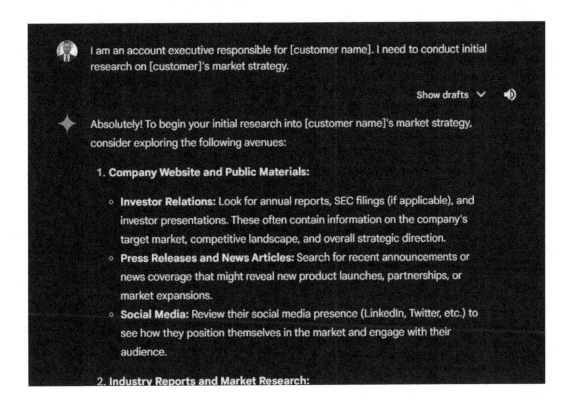

Gemini will provide initial insights to kickstart your research. To delve deeper, especially into recent developments, compile a list of relevant news URLs and query Gemini with:

✦ *"Summarize these articles from [URLs]. Provide key insights and explain the significance of these announcements."*

You now have a clear summary of the announcements, their significance, and further insights. To get a better understanding of the executive who will be your primary contact, you locate a recorded interview with them. You copy the YouTube URL into your session with Gemini at gemini.google.com and type:

- *"Summarize this interview from [URL] and provide insights about [executive name]. What are [executive]'s main concerns?"*

You now have a concise summary of the interview. To deepen your understanding of your key contact and the account, you continue the conversation by asking more targeted questions. You type into the prompt:

- *"Explain how [company] can assist [customer company] in achieving their goals."*

After concluding your conversation, you export the results to a Google Doc. You open the document and use Gemini in Docs to help draft your email. You enter:

- *"Draft an email for [customer] outlining why [your company] is the ideal partner to help them achieve their market goals."*

Prompt guide

Sales Manager
Use case: Develop customer relationships

As a Sales Manager, your annual conference is a key event to strengthen relationships with your most important customers and introduce prospects to your network. Here's how you can use Gemini in Google Workspace to enhance your engagement efforts:

Open Gmail and use Gemini by selecting "Help me write" and type the following prompt to create a personalized invitation:

- *"Draft an email inviting individuals interested in [focus area] to a happy hour at [trade show event] on [date, time]. Mention our specialization in [focus area]."*

Post-Event Follow-Up:

After the happy hour, continue the engagement by thanking the attendees. Open Gmail, select "Help me write," and enter:

- *"Compose a thank you email for attending our happy hour on [date, time, location]. Conclude with an invitation to continue the conversation in the coming weeks, maintaining a friendly tone."*

Gathering Feedback from Product Demos:

Following the event, gather valuable feedback from customers who participated in hands-on demo workshops. Open a new Google Doc, select "Help me write," and input:

"Create 10 survey questions to gather customer feedback on their experience with our [product/service]. Questions should assess the usefulness, highlights, and areas for improvement of [the product]."

This structured approach allows you to streamline communication and efficiently manage customer interactions using Gemini for Google Workspace, enhancing productivity and fostering deeper business relationships.

Use case: Support the sales team

When unexpected regional issues arise, providing clear and prompt guidance to your sales team is crucial. Here's how you can use Gemini in Google Workspace to effectively manage communication and mitigate customer concerns:

Open Gmail and activate Gemini by selecting "Help me write". Input the following prompt to draft an urgent message:

"Compose an email to all Northeast region sales leads. Outline the [issues] and instruct them to proactively inform their teams. Suggest offering customers a 20% discount on future orders as a goodwill gesture."

Coordinate Regional Team Meetings:

Still in Gmail, use the Gemini tool again by selecting "Help me write". Type this prompt to organize a crucial meeting:

"Draft an email to regional sales representatives to schedule an urgent meeting for next week regarding the [issues]. Request their availability for Monday or Tuesday and emphasize the importance of their feedback."

Use case: Coach and train the sales team

Recognizing the team's desire for more learning opportunities, you're planning a half-day educational program focused on your latest technology products. Here's how you can use Gemini in Google Workspace to streamline your planning:

Developing the Training Agenda:

Open a new Google Doc and activate Gemini by selecting "Help me write" and submitting the following prompt:

"Generate a half-day training agenda focused on our latest technology products for sales teams. Ensure the schedule includes a session by the product development team and allocates time for lunch."

Cataloging Learning Opportunities:

Following the training session, to better organize ongoing learning opportunities, open Google Sheets and prompt Gemini by selecting "Help me organize". Type this prompt:

"Create a spreadsheet listing online courses for sales personnel. Columns should include the course's main topic, cost, duration, and priority level."

Account Manager and Account Executive
Use case: Build customer relationships

After a productive discussion with a client, you decide to follow up by drafting a personalized email. You open the Google Doc containing your meeting notes and engage Gemini in Docs by selecting "Help me write". Write then the following prompt:

"Compose a personalized follow-up email to [client] summarizing our discussion. Include answers to any unresolved questions and reiterate the key points we covered."

Supporting New Service Onboarding:

With the customer starting to use a new service your company offers, it's crucial to ensure they receive ongoing support. To manage this, you decide to create a series of weekly check-in emails.Open a new Google Doc and use Gemini in Docs by selecting "Help me write" and using the following prompt:

"Draft four different weekly email templates to support my client who recentl y subscribed to our [service]. Each email should focus on a distinct value proposition—cost, ease of use, security, availability, or customization. Include a specific call to action in each message."

Use case: Prepare for new customer calls

Facing a new use case with a prospective client, you seek to prepare thoroughly for an upcoming video call. To begin, you visit gemini.google.com and input:

- *"Draft a detailed script for my upcoming 30-minute sales call with a prospect. Include how [company products/solutions] can alleviate the customer's specific pain points, details of our efficient delivery system, competitive pricing and bulk discounts, and a reference from a similar industry client."*

Compiling Research in a Google Doc:

After gathering initial insights, you transfer this information to a Google Doc to refine your strategy. With your research consolidated, you proceed to craft a tailored pitch by selecting "Help me write" and writing this prompt:

- *"Use the collected data to generate a compelling elevator pitch for [product name], focusing on its key benefits, unique selling points, and how it addresses specific customer challenges."*

Anticipating Customer Objections:

With the foundational pitch ready, you return to gemini.google.com to prepare for potential challenges during the call:

- *"I have an upcoming sales call with a prospect, focusing on a new use case. I need to prepare effectively, so please list the most common objections I might face from [customer] regarding [product]. Provide suggestions on how I can address these effectively. I operate in the [insert industry] and need strategic ways to handle and respond to any concerns."*

Business Development Manager
Use case: Nurture relationships, personalized outreach, and thought leadership

You aim to strengthen connections with potential customers you met at a recent business influencers networking event. To facilitate personalized communication, you decide to create a flexible email template. Open a new Google Doc, choose the "Help me write" function in Gemini for Docs and enter the following prompt:

- *"Create an email template for reaching out to industry influencers. Thank them for connecting at [event], and suggest possible collaborative efforts like [opportunities]."*

Following a productive discussion with prospective clients, you decide to engage them further with insightful content authored by your founder. To do this, you open a Google Doc containing the blog post and use the "Help me write" feature in Gemini for Docs. You then type:

"Summarize this blog post into key bullet points and develop three follow-up questions to encourage customers to share their thoughts."

Use case: Generate personalized customer onboarding materials

After successfully bringing on board several significant new clients, it's essential to maintain a warm and engaging relationship with them. To achieve this, you can utilize Gemini within Google Workspace for efficient and personalized communications.

You want to send a personalized thank-you email on the one-month anniversary of their partnership with your company. Start by launching your Gmail application, select the "Help me write" option provided by Gemini and enter the following prompt into Gemini:

"Craft a personalized thank-you email for [customer's name] to mark their one-month anniversary with [your company's name]. Include a message of gratitude, inquire if they need further assistance, and provide details about [another product/service] that might interest them."

Selecting a Congratulatory Gift

To further enhance your relationship with new clients, consider sending a thoughtful gift to celebrate the beginning of your partnership. Launch Google Sheets to organize and track your gift choices. Use the "Help me organize" feature in Gemini and input this prompt:

"Generate a list of potential client gifts under $200 each that can be delivered to offices, including gift options suitable for a corporate environment."

LEVELING UP YOUR PROMPT WRITING

This section of the guide is designed to further inspire and refine your prompt-writing abilities using Gemini for Google Workspace. While the foundational practices set a solid base, these advanced tips will help you unlock even greater potential and versatility in your interactions with Gemini.

Advanced Prompt Crafting Techniques

1. Segment Complex Tasks: When you need Gemini for Workspace to handle multiple related tasks, split these into separate prompts. This helps in managing complexity and ensures clarity in the responses you receive.

2. Specify Constraints: For more tailored results, define clear constraints in your prompts, such as character count limits or a specific number of options to generate. This guides Gemini to produce outputs that meet your exact needs.

3. Role Play to Boost Creativity: Inject creativity into your prompts by assigning a role to Gemini. Begin your prompt with a scenario, such as, "Imagine you are the head of a creative department at a top advertising agency..." This setup encourages Gemini to think within the context of that role, leading to more innovative ideas.

4. Engage in a Dialogue: Treat your interaction with Gemini as a collaborative project. Provide comprehensive details and state your expectations clearly. Enhance the interaction by asking open-ended questions like, "What additional information do you need to deliver the best results?" This approach makes the AI a more active participant in achieving the desired outcome.

5. Adjust Tone According to Audience: Always consider the tone of your content. Specify whether you need a formal, informal, technical, creative, or casual tone to ensure the output resonates with your target audience.

6. Iterative Refinement: If the initial results from Gemini don't fully meet your expectations, don't hesitate to refine your prompts. An iterative process where you tweak and adjust your requests can significantly enhance the quality and relevance of the responses.

By incorporating these advanced strategies into your prompt-writing practices, you'll be able to leverage Gemini for Google Workspace more effectively, ensuring that every interaction moves you closer to your operational goals. Whether you're streamlining communication, fostering creativity, or enhancing productivity, these tips will empower you and your team to excel.

SHARE YOUR INSIGHTS

Would you spare a moment to impact someone's professional growth? Your knowledge and feedback are invaluable.

Currently, there are professionals, mentors, and leaders who are enhancing their skills and overcoming challenges. Your review could serve as a critical resource for them.

Reviews are more than just feedback; they are endorsements, shared wisdom, and a measure of trust. If you've gained actionable insights or innovative ideas from this book, please share your thoughts through a quick review. Your contribution supports:

- Guiding others to tools and strategies that enhance their leadership abilities.
- Helping individuals improve their mentoring and coaching skills.
- Broadening someone's perspective, which could be transformative.
- Inspiring changes that propel professional journeys forward.

By reviewing this book, you help expand the scope of effective leadership, mentorship, and coaching. If this book was helpful, consider recommending it to your network. The value you share can leave a lasting impression.

If you enjoyed our book, use the QR code to leave a review where you purchased it. Your feedback is crucial!

Thank you for endorsing the path to impactful leadership and personal development.

Best regards,

Mauricio

Unlock FREE 70+ Exclusive Gemini Prompts for Business and Life

Dive into our exclusive FREE collection of 70+ Gemini prompts tailored for enhancing productivity and decision-making in both business and personal settings. These prompts are ready to use, adaptable, and cover many scenarios to meet your needs.

Access these valuable tools now by scanning the QR code below and start transforming your business!

www.ingramcontent.com/pod-product-compliance
Lightning Source LLC
La Vergne TN
LVHW082034050326
832904LV00006B/281

* 9 7 8 1 9 9 8 4 0 2 3 3 5 *